D0893522

Mikhail Lermontov

Twayne's World Authors Series

Charles A. Moser, Editor of Russian Literature

George Washington University

TWAS 667

*Lermontov in the uniform of
the Life Guard Hussars, painted
in oils by Zabolotsky (1837).*

Mikhail Lermontov

By John Garrard

University of Virginia

Twayne Publishers • Boston

Mikhail Lermontov

John Garrard

Copyright © 1982 by G. K. Hall & Company
All Rights Reserved
Published by Twayne Publishers
A Division of G. K. Hall & Company
70 Lincoln Street
Boston, Massachusetts 02111

Book Production by Marne B. Sultz
Book Design by Barbara Anderson

Printed on permanent/durable acid-free
paper and bound in The United States
of America.

Library of Congress Cataloging in Publication Data

Garrard, John Gordon.
  Mikhail Lermontov.

  (Twayne's world authors series ; TWAS 667)
  Bibliography: p. 158
  Includes index.
    1. Lermontov, Mikhail IUrévich, 1814–1841—Critic-
ism and interpretation. I. Title. II. Series.
PG3337.L46G3   891.71′3   82–6194
ISBN 0–8057–6514–X   AACR2

*Dedicated
with love and admiration
to my mother and father*

Contents

About the Author

John G. Garrard received the B.A. from Oxford University in England and the Ph.D. from Columbia University in New York. He is the author of books and articles about eighteenth-, nineteenth-, and twentieth-century Russian literature. He has taught at Dartmouth College and Indiana University as well as the University of Virginia, where he is now professor of Russian literature and director of the Center for Russian and East European Studies.

Preface

Mikhail Yurievich Lermontov is one of those rare writers who achieve equal distinction in both prose fiction and poetry. His best-known work is *A Hero of Our Time* (1840), the first great psychological novel in Russian literature. But he also wrote three famous narrative poems, one of which is certainly a masterpiece, and some of the most beautiful lyrics in the Russian language. He is regarded as the second poet, after Alexander Pushkin, in Russian literature. Lermontov was not only a great writer but also a gifted musician and painter. Many of his paintings and sketches of the Caucasus display genuine talent. Yet he never became a professional writer or artist. From the age of eighteen he served in the Life Guard Hussars; he demonstrated such exceptional bravery in hand-to-hand fighting against Caucasian tribesmen that his commanding officer recommended that he be awarded the rare honor of a gold saber inscribed simply "For Courage." Lermontov packed all this activity into a very short life: he was killed in a pistol duel at twenty-six.

Even though Lermontov is recognized as a writer of the first rank, surprisingly little has been published on him in English. The present book is in fact the first full-length English-language study of his life and the entire spectrum of his works in both poetry and prose. Soviet scholars have published the primary sources and other biographical and archival materials having to do with his life. Very little of this been translated, however, and beyond that the evaluation and interpretation of the primary sources by Soviet scholars is frequently open to question.

This book is intended to provide the reader with a balanced appraisal of all Lermontov's works, viewed against the background of his life and his cultural and social milieu. I have therefore drawn heavily upon primary sources: Lermontov's poetry and prose, his letters (mostly written in French), and the memoirs of his contemporaries. For *A Hero of Our Time* I have used the widely accepted translation by Vladimir and Dmitri Nabokov. Translations of all other French and Russian materials are my own.

Lermontov wrote during the 1830s, when Russian literature was in transition from a great age of poetry to a great age of prose. This movement is faithfully reflected in his works. He perfects, and in the process exhausts, many poetic themes, styles, and forms. But in prose fiction he lays the foundation for the great psychological novels of Dostoevsky and Tolstoy. Grigory Pechorin, in *A Hero of Our Time,* remains one of the most dynamic and enigmatic figures in all of Russian fiction.

Lermontov's writing also reflects his own contradictory personality. He was heavily influenced by the English poet George Gordon, Lord Byron, a literary relationship I have traced over the course of his brief life. And I have treated Lermontov's works for the most part in the chronological order of their composition, not publication.

Lermontov's literary activity spanned a dozen years, which may be divided into three periods of four years each. The first two are periods of apprenticeship. He spent 1828 to 1832 in Moscow, first at school and then at the university. In 1832 he moved to St. Petersburg to begin his military career. Lermontov's mature period begins with his poem on the death of Pushkin, killed in a duel in late January 1837, and closes with Lermontov's own death in July 1841. By an extraordinary coincidence, the two greatest poets in Russian literature died in pistol duels a few years apart.

Chapter 1 contains an outline of Lermontov's life and literary career. Chapter 2 includes a discussion of the narrative poems, plays, and lyrical poetry written from 1828 to 1832 in Moscow. Chapter 3 examines his narrative poems, notably *The Boyar Orsha,* the unfinished historical novel *Vadim,* and *Masquerade,* the only one of Lermontov's five plays to have survived the test of time. In Chapter 4 I analyze representative lyrics from Lermontov's mature period, the poems which justify Lermontov's reputation as one of the greatest poets in Russian. Chapter 5 contains a discussion of his narrative poems: *The Demon, The Novice, Sashka, The Tambov Treasurer's Wife, The Merchant Kalashnikov,* and the unfinished *A Fairy Tale for Children.* Chapter 6 begins with a brief review of his unfinished novel *Princess Ligovskaya,* then proceeds to a detailed analysis of *A Hero of Our Time.* Chapter 7 sums up the chief characteristics of Lermontov's works, placing him in the context of Russian literature and the society of his own time.

I have not had space in this book to review all the literature on Lermontov, but I have tried to place Boris Eykhenbaum's reputation as a Lermontov specialist in a more balanced perspective. Eykhenbaum's position as a scholar is of course secure, but he clearly owes many of his insights into Lermontov's works to a seminal article published in 1914, in Russian, by Vladimir Fisher. Eykhenbaum's famous book of 1924 must be viewed, I believe, as an expansion of ideas advanced by Fisher ten years before. Fisher's article has been totally ignored by Soviet scholarship and has never been reprinted or translated. American writers on Lermontov seem quite unaware of its existence.

Notes to the Reader:
1. All dates quoted are given according to the Julian Calendar, used in Russia until 1918. In the nineteenth century the Julian Calendar was twelve days behind the Gregorian Calendar, which was already in use in Western Europe and the United States.
2. Every Russian has three names: a given name, a patronymic (formed from the given name of the father), and a surname. So, for example, Mikhail Yurievich (son of Yury) Lermontov.
3. Russians used to celebrate their "name-days" rather than their birthdays. The Russian Orthodox Church, like the Catholic Church, has a liturgical calender for the commemoration of saints. A Russian celebrated the day of the saint after whom he was named as his "name-day."

John Garrard

University of Virginia

Acknowledgments

I am chiefly indebted to my wife, Carol, who read and typed all my drafts and made many valuable suggestions for their improvement. It is a simple fact that the book would never have been written without her encouragement, and whatever merits it may possess are in large part due to her help.

I am deeply grateful for research support to the Russian Institute of Columbia University and its then director William E. Harkins for the opportunity to use the magnificent Columbia University Library while I was a research associate of the institute; to the Rockefeller Foundation for an idyllic month spent writing in the peace and quiet of the Villa Serbelloni at Bellagio, Italy; and to IREX for the chance to do research in Moscow and Leningrad and to consult with Russian Lermontov specialists who gave generously of their time and vast knowledge: V. A. Manuylov, V. E. Vatsuro, I. S. Chistova, and I. Usok.

I am grateful to Harcourt Brace Jovanovich, Inc. for permission to quote from *English Romantic Writers,* edited by David Perkins (1967).

My special thanks go to Charles A. Moser, Editor of the Russian Section of TWAS, and to Faith M. Kaliski, Assistant Editor, and Marne B. Sultz, Production Editor at G. K. Hall & Co., for the great care and skill they brought to editing and producing this book.

The index was compiled by Dr. Madhu Malik.

Any faults and errors that remain are my responsibility.

Chronology

1839   August 5: dates manuscript of *The Novice*. December 6: promoted from cornet to lieutenant.

1840   February 18: inconclusive duel with Ernest de Barante, son of French ambassador. April 13: transferred without loss of rank for dueling to Tenginsky Infantry Regiment in the Caucasus. April: *A Hero of Our Time* published. Early May: leaves St. Petersburg. May 9: attends name-day party for Gogol in Moscow. June 10: arrives in Stavropol, H.Q. of General Grabbe. Summer and fall: displays great courage in action against Caucasian tribesmen; recommended for medals and gold saber for valor. October 25: collection of poetry published.

1841   February 5: arrives in St. Petersburg on leave. April 14: leaves for the Caucasus. May: *A Hero of Our Time* (2d edition) published. May 20: arrives in Pyatigorsk. July 15: killed in pistol duel by Nikolay Martynov.

Chapter One
"Mad, Bad, and Dangerous to Know"

Mikhail Yurievich Lermontov was born in the early morning hours of 3 October 1814 in Moscow. His father Yury Petrovich, who had taken an early medical retirement from the army, was a handsome, sociable, but short-tempered man. Family legend had it that the Lermontovs were descended from Spanish ancestors who had later moved to Scotland and then entered Russian service. Such claims to foreign and/or ancient lineage in Russia were frequently little more than a genteel cover for lack of present wealth and distinction.[1] Still, Yury Petrovich succeeded in parlaying his undoubted good looks and supposed ancestry into a very advantageous marriage with Maria Mikhaylovna Arsenieva, a member of the truly distinguished Stolypin family, which disapproved of him. In contrast to her husband, Maria Mikhaylovna was not only rich, but also quite plain in appearance. She was also sickly, and died of consumption in early 1817, before her twenty-second birthday, when Lermontov was only two and a half years old.

The brief, unequal marriage seems not to have been a success, certainly not in the eyes of the bride's mother, Elizaveta Alekseevna Arsenieva (née Stolypina). Even before her daughter's untimely death Mme Arsenieva made little effort to conceal either her disapproval of Yury Petrovich or her firm intention of playing the central role in her grandson's upbringing. She brought the family to live at her estate, Tarkhany (now renamed Lermontovo), located about 350 miles east-southeast of Moscow in Penza Province.

Mme Arsenieva was a strong-willed woman, but Yury Petrovich made his mother-in-law pay dearly for having her way. On two occasions—shortly after Lermontov's birth and again after his mother's death—Mme Arsenieva signed promissory notes guaranteeing Yury Petrovich the princely sum of 25,000 rubles. She was required to hand over the money within one year each time, and only managed to do so by borrowing heavily from relatives, since most of her wealth was in the form of real property and serfs. Her agreement with Yury Petrovich also required her to make Lermontov her sole heir. This she was probably happy to do, having no children of her own.

In return for these commitments, Yury Petrovich left Tarkhany shortly after his wife's death and agreed not to come back. He went to live in his modest house in Tula Province south of Moscow, reportedly drinking and wenching until 1831, when he too died of tuberculosis at the age of forty-four.

In an age when good family connections and a privileged background contributed much to a young person's chances for success, Yury Petrovich had made a sensible, if cold-blooded, decision. He could not hope to bring up his son in the manner his mother-in-law could, and he had assured his son's future at no cost to himself.

Lermontov went to visit his father briefly at Kropotovo in the late summer of 1827, and in the fall of 1828 Yury Petrovich came to see his son at school in Moscow. Apart from these visits Lermontov appears to have seen little of his father, but he did witness some very unedifying arguments between his father and grandmother regarding his custody and upbringing, which find an obvious echo in his play of 1830, *Menschen und Leidenschaften* [People and Passions—the German title is Lermontov's].

Much has been written about the nature of Lermontov's relationship with his father and its impact upon his personality. In the play just mentioned, though, the father is portrayed favorably and the grandmother comes across as a harridan, while Yury Volin (i.e., Lermontov himself) is an idealized young man who sides with his father.

Immediately upon learning of his father's death in 1831, Lermontov wrote a poem beginning:

> It is a terrible fate for father and son
> To live separately and to die apart.[2]

Lermontov goes on to suggest that he has been the cause of all his father's "torments," and says:

> It is not for me to judge whether you are guilty or not;
> You are condemned by society? But what is society?

Lermontov does not say why society should have condemned his father.

If the father-son relationship appears affectionate here, in later works of Lermontov's the father figure is often portrayed negatively. For example, in *Stranny chelovek* [The Strange Man], a play he wrote in 1831 even before his father died, Lermontov portrays himself again as an idealized, misunderstood young man whose father treats both him and his mother callously. Later, in the comic narrative poem *Sashka* (1835–36), the fourteen-year-old hero wins out over his degenerate father for the affections of a housemaid. In this unfinished work, neither father nor son is very admirable, and the strong implication is that Sashka goes wrong because he is badly treated by his father (his mother has died young).

From all this it would seem that Lermontov, not knowing his father well, at first discounted the gossip about his father's drinking bouts and frequent sorties among the serf girls, but later concluded it was true. He may also have heard rumors that his father treated his mother harshly, even physically abused her. It must be stressed, however, that we have no direct evidence as to Lermontov's feelings, and adducing them from his writing is a tricky business at best.

In 1830 Lermontov recorded the only memory he had of his mother:

When I was two, there was a song that made me cry. I cannot remember it now, but I am sure that, if I heard it again, it would have the same effect. My mother sang it to me. (4:352)

The date of this note may be significant, for in 1830 Lermontov had just discovered Byron. It is possible that, encouraged by the English poet's example, he was "creating" examples of early sensitivity. What is more, fifteen is an impressionable age; Lermontov, newly aware of himself as a person, was trying to come to terms with his family situation. He had been surrounded by servants who saw to his every need. Raised in this hothouse atmosphere, he had become thoroughly absorbed in himself and acquired an exaggerated opinion of the significance of his own thoughts and emotions. Certainly his mother's early death and the peculiar departure of his father must have upset him, and supplied material for his self-projection as a lonely, unloved youth, an image which constantly recurs in his poetry.

Early Upbringing

Although deprived of the joys of family life, Lermontov had a happy childhood. Akim Shan-Girey, one of his countless cousins and four years his junior, spent two years (1825–27) with him at Tarkhany. In his memoirs, written in 1860, he recalled Lermontov as a cheerful, normal boy with a special talent for building magnificent snowmen "of a colossal size."[3]

But Lermontov had other aptitudes of a more intellectual nature. He had great emotional energy which he poured into music, drawing, and painting. He became very early an accomplished painter and singer, and played both the piano and the violin well. For the Romantics music was the supreme art, and Lermontov remained throughout his life passionately fond of it. This special relationship to music is reflected later both in the preferences of his major heroes and in the uniquely melodic quality of his verse.

As was the custom in those days among aristocratic families of Europe, Lermontov received his early education at home from private tutors, one of whom was a former French officer from Napoleon's Grande Armée who had decided to remain in Russia after being wounded and taken prisoner in 1812.

Mme Arsenieva spared no expense to insure that little Michel received an excellent grounding in what we call the liberal arts, for she evidently intended that her sole heir should have a brilliant career. By 1827 she had decided to take him to Moscow to continue his education somewhat more intensively. There he was coached by special tutors in preparation for the entrance examination of the Moscow University School for the Nobility. After continuing his lessons through the winter, Lermontov spent the summer at Tarkhany, then returned to Moscow to enter the School on 1 September 1828.

At almost fourteen, Lermontov must have found attending an all-boys school a jolt. He had been brought up mostly by adoring women and devoted servants. Apart from his cousin Shan-Girey, he had had no male friends. On the other hand, he had fallen in love at least twice with girls. One of his autobiographical notes of 1830 tells of his first love at the age of ten. The object of his passion was a girl of nine, a friend of the family: "Once, I remember, I ran into a room: she was there playing dolls with my cousin: my heart beat faster and my knees shook . . ." (4:351). In a note added sometime later to a poem of 1829, Lermontov recalled his second affair of the heart, which occurred in Kropotovo in 1827 (1:545).

Even though she had enrolled him at an all-boys school, Mme Arsenieva continued to shelter him, insisting he be only a semi-boarder and return home every day after classes to sleep. Lermontov was not the first child to find it difficult to make friends in such circumstances. A memoirist recalls that Lermontov tried to make friends, but was not popular, and even somehow earned the nickname "Frog" (*Vosp.,* 110).

The one thing that distinguished Lermontov at the School for Nobility was his precocious skill at writing poetry. This interest was encouraged by the school's curriculum, which stressed foreign languages, including Latin and Greek, and the reading and translation of poetry. His several translations and adaptations, chiefly from English and German, as well as his own early poetic efforts, were undoubtedly inspired by his school work, and may in some cases have been assignments. In 1829 Lermontov made translations (sometimes partial) and adaptations of the lyrics and ballads of Friedrich Schiller, but he was even more impressed by Schiller's plays, with their melodramatic, highly wrought calls for personal and social freedom. Schiller's *Die Räuber* [The Robbers] had a profound influence on Lermontov's own early attempts at drama.

A further outlet for Lermontov's poetic interests was the school's literary magazine, in which several of his pieces appeared.

Thus Lermontov at this stage of his life was a fairly common adolescent type: a boy, from a wealthy but broken home, sheltered in a hothouse atmosphere by female relatives, who satisfies his need for emotional warmth by reading, playing music, and writing poetry. He joined a literary group and wrote for the school magazine, thus establishing a niche for himself. But his emotional maximalism—his intensity and desire for immediate deep friendships—repelled many of his contemporaries.

Whatever his problems making friends at school, at home Lermontov was surrounded by well-disposed relatives and friends of both sexes. Not only Akim Shan-Girey and his family, but also the Bakhmetevs, Lopukhins, and countless Stolypins were in his circle. It seems as though in Moscow society of those times almost everyone was related, however distantly, to everyone else.

Among Lermontov's close friends at this time was Svyatoslav Raevsky, Mme Arsenieva's godson. He lived at Tarkhany for several years as a boy, and, although six years older, became Lermontov's lifelong friend. Lermontov also maintained a warm relationship throughout his life with Aleksey Lopukhin, and with Aleksey's sisters, Maria and Elizaveta. Maria was twelve years older than Lermontov and clearly served him as a surrogate mother. Of the very few Lermontov letters that have come down to us, those to Maria are the most important and revealing.

The youngest Lopukhin sister, Varvara, had been living at the family's country estate in Tula Province. In the fall of 1831, when she was fifteen, she arrived in Moscow to be introduced into society. Though no great beauty, she attracted Lermontov at once by her gentleness and naturally kind disposition. After returning from her name-day party on 2 December, he wrote himself a rather puzzled note: "Yesterday once again I marveled at the duration of my happiness! Who would have thought, looking at her, that she could become the cause of suffering?" (4:354). The symbiotic relationship between love and suffering is, of course, a favorite Romantic paradox, but for Lermontov it was much more than a literary device. He was unlucky in love and believed that he always would be: fate had ordained it.

Lermontov had a large number of cousins, mostly girls, who in turn introduced him to their friends, so that his circle of female acquaintances became quite wide. He could meet girls socially through the year, and on a more long-term basis during the summer vacations, spent in 1829 and 1830 at the magnificent Stolypin estate of Serednikovo outside Moscow. In 1830 he fell seriously in love for the first time with Ekaterina Aleksandrovna Sushkova. She had recently become the close friend of one of Lermontov's relations, Aleksandra Mikhaylovna Vereshchagina.

Sushkova's memoirs of her relationship with Lermontov, though containing minor errors of fact, provide a valuable picture of his behavior and attitudes, not only in 1830 but also later in St. Petersburg in 1834–35, when she and Lermontov met again. For once, an addressee of Lermontov's love poems talks back. She describes Lermontov as "a clumsy, awkward boy of about sixteen or seventeen, with pretty, but intelligent, expressive eyes, a snub-nose, and sarcastic mocking smile" (*Vosp.,* 82–83). Lermontov tried to appear self-assured around her, but in vain.

In the summer of 1830 Aleksandra and Ekaterina traveled from their summer homes to Serednikovo to attend Mass each Sunday and then stay the whole day. The girls were both older than Lermontov (the first by four years, the second by two). But there was more than a difference in age; there was a difference in experience. The young women regarded Lermontov as a boy; Sushkova called him "Michel," a form of address commonly used with a child.

"This treatment made him extremely angry," she wrote. "He tried desperately to make us regard him as a young man; he recited to us Pushkin, Lamartine, and was never without the great Byron" (*Vosp.* 84).

So the summer passed with Lermontov acting as the ladies' cavalier, trying vainly to draw them into "very sentimental discussions" and assuring Sushkova of the significance of a first love. After a time Sushkova began to talk more seriously with Lermontov. She had early recognized his great intelligence, and now began using the adult form of address, Mikhail Yurievich, rather than Michel. She also discussed, critically but constructively, the poems he addressed to her; and she says he was very grateful for her suggestions.

In August of 1830 Lermontov and his grandmother left Serednikovo for Moscow. He was scheduled now to enter Moscow University, rather than the School for the Nobility. This change in plans had come about after a visit by Tsar Nicholas I to the school the previous spring. The Tsar had arrived unannounced and chanced to enter the school building during recess, when the boys were noisily running through the corridors without any apparent supervision. Nicholas was outraged by this unseemly behavior. Attributing it to the relative freedom the school enjoyed due to its special status, Nicholas ordered its curriculum emasculated and had the institution itself downgraded to a simple *gimnaziya,* or ordinary school. This was a sad and sudden decline for an institution which had played a significant role in the cultural development of Russia since its founding in 1779.

Mme Arsenieva had decided at once that there was no point in Lermontov's remaining at such an institution and obtained permission for him to leave. He continued his studies privately in preparation for the entrance examination to Moscow University, which he passed without difficulty.

At the University

On 1 September 1830, Lermontov registered for classes, but hardly had time to settle in when an unusually virulent cholera epidemic swept up from the south to Moscow, and the university was closed down.[4]

With no need to attend classes, Lermontov saw a great deal of Sushkova, as well as other friends and acquaintances in society. He developed into a witty and entertaining dinner companion, and was the life of the party when guests began to play games and charades. He had also started to turn his rhyming skill to the composition of epigrams, and could produce remarkably diverting impromptu verses on almost any subject. His wit made him the center of attention, and that increased his self-confidence.

Lermontov was particularly adept at a poetic genre quite popular in his own time, but today completely forgotten: album verse. Young ladies in Europe of the 1830s kept albums in which they invited friends and special visitors to contribute greetings, witticisms (traditionally in verse), sketches, or even paintings. Lermontov wrote many poems in albums; indeed, some of his poems have only survived in the albums in which he originally wrote them. Happily, the album belonging to Sashenka Vereshchagina, containing many of Lermontov's drawings and verses, is extant in the library of Columbia University.

Lermontov's ability to write witty and entertaining verse allowed him to move with increasing self-assurance in society. One of his most notable social triumphs is recorded in the memoirs of Shan-Girey. On New Year's Eve in 1831, Lermontov appeared at a masquerade held at the Assembly of the Nobility dressed as an astrologer and carrying a huge book covered with Chinese characters. The book contained, in the form of horoscopes, a series of short poems about various friends whom he and Shan-Girey expected to meet at the masquerade. Shan-Girey had cut the Chinese characters out of black paper (*Vosp.*, 37).

Lermontov's mock horoscopes had no literary merit, but the list of addressees provides a useful guide to the Moscow society he frequented. The list includes an important government official, a famous beauty and a lady-in-waiting to the Empress, a well-known female singer, and the daughter of a senator, whose home was a central meeting place for the cream of Moscow society as well as for writers and musicians. In an odd twist of fate, Lermontov addressed one horoscope to a sister of Nikolay Martynov, the man who would kill him ten years later.

On New Year's Eve in 1831 Lermontov was still only seventeen, but he had already begun to make a name for himself in society, and he was clearly determined to become a social lion. In her memoirs, Sushkova tells us she finally realized "how full [Lermontov's] head was of romantic notions and how early he had conceived the desire to become a hero and breaker of female hearts." She speaks of his "excessive pride," adding this revealing comment:

Ever since his early youth he had been tormented by the fact that he was unattractive, ungainly, and not of distinguished background [on his father's side]. In moments of enthusiasm he confessed to me several times that he wanted to become *somebody,* but—and this was important—he planned to make it by himself and not be indebted to anyone else for his success. (*Vosp.,* 96)

Sushkova had parted with Lermontov in October 1830, accompanied by his poems of regret and despair, at the time of the cholera epidemic, and her place in Lermontov's heart as beloved and chief tormenter was taken by Natalya Fyodorovna Ivanova. She was the addressee of the first mock horoscope at the New Year's Eve ball, and the only one whose name was omitted in later manuscript copies prepared by or for Lermontov. Her initials occur at the head of a large number of poems Lermontov wrote throughout 1831 and the early part of 1832. He concealed Ivanova's name because she married not long afterward, and her husband was extremely jealous of her earlier friendship with him. In fact, he burned a box of letters and poems Lermontov had written her.

Lermontov had as little success in his "affair" with Natalya Ivanova as he had had with Ekaterina Sushkova. He was still too demanding and intense, and too inexperienced. He spent a few days at the Ivanov country estate in June 1831, but his stay only produced more poems complaining of Natalya's inconstancy and of his own accursed fate.

It is clear that Lermontov was leading a full social life, unimpeded by his minimal obligations as a student at Moscow University. When classes resumed in early 1831, Lermontov was most selective about which ones he attended, for he was already highly educated and thought he knew considerably more than most of the professors.

Not only was his academic work unchallenging for him, his interests now lay elsewhere: in poetry and in the social whirl. If earlier in his school days he had been unsure of himself, now he felt no need to prove himself among fellow students. His isolation from his fellow students has been much lamented by Soviet scholars. He did not join any of the circles formed at about this time to discuss the ideas of Hegel and Schelling, or the French Utopian Socialists. He never even met such fellow students as Ivan Goncharov, later an important novelist; Vissarion Belinsky, who became the most famous Russian literary critic of the nineteenth century; or Alexander Herzen, the noted liberal who fled Russia and eventually founded the anti-Tsarist journal *Kolokol* [The Bell]. While Lermontov was completely aware of the ideas in circulation, sitting down to discuss them simply was not his style.[5]

The few memoirs written by his contemporaries at the university are agreed that Lermontov was distant and unfriendly. They also support Sushkova's recollection of his appearance as "an awkward, round-shouldered, short young fellow of about sixteen, with black hair, an olive-colored face, and large black eyes that looked at you sullenly" (Ya. I. Kostenetsky in *Vosp.*, 261).[6] All concur that his only striking feature were his large expressive eyes, which intimidated anyone who disturbed or irritated him.

This was not hard to do, for Lermontov had by now become not only an intellectual but a social snob. He stressed his supposed Spanish origins, signing himself "Lerma" or "Lermantov" for several years. He was delighted to find a character called Lerma in Schiller's *Don Carlos,* set in Spain during the Inquisition. He even painted a portrait of himself as a Spanish grandee.

Indeed, Lermontov was so snobbish that he would even pretend not to notice fellow students when attending social functions away from the university. A contemporary, Pavel Vistengof, saw him regularly at the brilliant Tuesday-evening balls held at the Moscow Assembly of the Nobility. Lermontov pretended not to know him even though they both attended the same classes at Moscow University. Without rancor, Vistengof describes Lermontov as always elegantly dressed and surrounded by attractive young ladies of the highest society, although he never danced. It was clear to Vistengof that Lermontov had excellent social connections and that he enjoyed considerable wealth.

Vistengof's memoirs also recount an incident that reveals another aspect of Lermontov's personality not normally visible to chance acquaintances at Moscow University. Lermontov led not only a separate social existence but also an intensely private intellectual and cultural life. Vistengof recalls Lermontov as a silent, gloomy fellow: "He always used to sit in the same place all by himself in the corner of the auditorium by the window, leaning on one elbow, totally absorbed in some book that he had brought with him; he never paid any attention to the lectures" (*Vosp.*, 103). On one occasion Vistengof accepted a dare from friends who were thoroughly puzzled by Lermontov's behavior. When he asked Lermontov what he was reading so avidly, Vistengof was rewarded with an icy stare and told that Lermontov had no intention of wasting time explaining the contents of a book to someone who was quite incapable of understanding it. Vistengof adds: "I recoiled as though stung and had time only to glance for an instant at the book: it was in English." Almost certainly, the book was by George Gordon, Lord Byron.

Lermontov and Byron

At that time Lermontov discovered Byron as a poet and as a person. The two aspects were intimately linked in Byron, as they were in Lermontov, whose early fascination with Byronism and its demonic variant was stimulated in 1830 by the publication by Byron's friend Thomas Moore of *Letters and Journals of Lord Byron*. The book was immediately translated into French and thus became available to Lermontov, who obviously read it avidly, delighted to discover the manifold similarities between himself and his hero.

Direct evidence of the impact of Byron's letters and journals on the young Lermontov is provided by the series of autobiographical notes he wrote in 1830 to which reference has already been made. Among them is a touchingly naive note in which he proudly mentions "yet another similarity between my life and that of Lord Byron." He had read in Moore that an old woman in Scotland had told Byron's mother that he would be a great man and marry twice, and apparently an old woman in the Caucasus had prophesied exactly the same fate for him to his grandmother: "God grant that really happens to me too, even though I become just as unhappy as Byron" (4:353).

Lermontov's reading of Byron's letters and journals encouraged him to turn much more often to the Englishman's poetry. For example, he imitated Byron's "Hebrew Melodies" in his poem "Evreyskaya melodiya" [Hebrew Melody], which begins "Once I saw the evening star"; and he did a prose translation of Byron's "Darkness."

But the significance of Moore's book is not limited to such literary influences. Lermontov also saw in Byron a model as a man. In a poem entitled enigmatically "K***" [To . . .], to which he added a note: "After reading the life of Byron by Moore," he states bravely that no one need pity him; he knows that he has even heavier burdens to bear in the future. In the remaining three stanzas of the four-stanza poem Lermontov compares himself directly with Byron: "Our souls are the same, and so are our torments; / If only our fates could be similar!" (1:125). What Lermontov meant by "fate" (or "destiny") is anybody's guess; perhaps he hoped to share Byron's fame, since he hated the thought that he might die unknown. In addition, he may have had in mind Byron's death at Missolonghi, after the English poet caught fever trying to aid the Greek struggle for independence: the third stanza, after the lines quoted above, begins: "Like him I seek oblivion and freedom." The oblivion Lermontov seeks is forgetfulness of past torments. The Byronic hero habitually, but unsuccessfully, seeks an emotional and moral limbo, a twilight zone where he can drift happily, quite indifferent to either good or evil.

Lermontov's fascination with Byron continued in 1831 and the first half of 1832, during his university days. His discovery of Byron's personality, the facts of his childhood and upbringing, contributed to Lermontov's growing self-confidence. The parallels he found between himself and Byron enabled Lermontov to establish a new genealogy to replace the suspect one he had been born with. He also acquired a new self-image to protect him from disappointments and rebuffs, one which would serve him as a springboard for the creation of his poetic persona, his lyrical hero.

The St. Petersburg Period

Suddenly, in June 1832, Lermontov obtained a transcript from Moscow University in order to transfer to the University of St. Petersburg. In his request for it, he stated that he could not remain at Moscow because of "family circumstances." To this day no one knows precisely what prompted Lermontov's decision to leave Moscow for St. Petersburg, a city he never liked, and compared unfavorably to Moscow. There are some plausible conjectures as to the reason. Lermontov, according to several reports, behaved in a supercilious manner not only with other students, but also with members of the faculty, and apparently insulted at least one professor. Perhaps he feared they might seek revenge, and so he did not even take the final examinations at the end of the 1831–32 academic year. He did, however, withdraw in good standing.

There may have been other reasons for his departure. His relationship with Natalya Ivanova had come to a wrenching end when she apparently told him that she loved someone else. Also, it is possible that Lermontov wanted to stay near his close friends and relatives, many of whom were now moving to St. Petersburg to enter Tsarist Russia's equivalent of West Point, the School of Guards Ensign Cadets and Cavalry Hussars.

The career options of young aristocrats were, in fact, severely limited. Andrey Miklashevsky, a fellow student of Lermontov's at the School for the Nobility, who also moved to St. Petersburg in 1832, makes this point:

At the end of the 1820s and the very beginning of the 1830s the only career open to young men who had completed their education was military service. Law schools did not as yet exist, and all civil servants were called pen-pushers [*podyachie*]. (*Vosp.*, 111)

Miklashevsky is speaking here from the point of view of the landed gentry, with its aristocratic disdain for anyone who worked for a living.

This situation must have been as clear to Lermontov and his grandmother as it was to all the other young men who moved to the St. Petersburg military schools and academies.

When the University of St. Petersburg refused to grant him credit for his studies in Moscow, Lermontov immediately applied for admission to the military academy. He took the entrance examination on 4 November, and was assigned as a cadet to the Life Guard Hussar Regiment on 10 November. Russia's army at that time was divided into infantry and cavalry regiments, with the latter made up of the social elite. Lermontov's assignment to a cavalry regiment rather than to the infantry is a testament less to his intellectual ability than to his high social connections.

No doubt Mme Arsenieva had much to do with his assignment, for even in October Lermontov seemed quite confident he would join the cavalry. He wrote to Sashenka Vereshchagina: "You must already know, my lady, that I am entering the Guards School" (4:376), so he seemed to know how things were done then, for he made this statement even before taking his entrance exam.

During the fall Lermontov had plenty of time to do some writing and to engage in fairly extensive correspondence with his Moscow friends. Understandably, he felt a little lonely and perhaps apprehensive about the immediate future. In sending a poem to a close family friend, Sofia Bakhmeteva (fourteen years his senior), Lermontov commented that for some unknown reason "the poetry of my soul has died." Then he added: "By the way, if I had started writing to you an hour sooner, then perhaps I would have written something quite different; every moment I have new fantasies" (4:366).

Lermontov apparently did little socializing at this time; perhaps most people were still away at their summer homes. In any case he wrote on 28 August to Maria Lopukhina: "Me, that is the person whose company I most enjoy." Later in the same letter he remarks:

I write little, and read not at all; my novel has become a work of despair; I have rummaged around my soul gathering everything that could be turned into hatred—and I have poured it all out on paper: you would pity me if you read it! (4:367)

This further mention of his difficulties in writing indicates that the move to St. Petersburg had disrupted his poetic and psychological life. And his mention of a novel is the first reference in his correspondence or in the memoirs of the period to an actual project in prose fiction. Shortly thereafter he was writing an historical romance set during the Pugachev Rebellion of the 1770s, and it is quite possible that he is speaking of that here.

Another letter from Lermontov to Maria Lopukhina of 2 September reveals that he missed Moscow but was still anxious to make a name for himself in the capital. Later in the same letter he says: "It is terrible to think that the day will come when I can no longer say 'I'! At that thought the whole world becomes nothing but a clod of earth" (4:371).

Lermontov wrote far less over the next four years than he had in his Moscow period. There is a particularly noticeable dearth of lyric poetry during what is generally called his "Hussar period": evidently the lyric impulse dried up under the pressure of barracks life. Suddenly, after mooning over flirtatious cousins and their friends, Lermontov began frequenting whorehouses. Instead of love lyrics expressing undying devotion he started writing what Russian scholars call delicately "Hussar poems" (*yunkerskie poemy*). These are scabrous, at times mildly pornographic accounts of various amorous adventures which he and his fellow cadets had enjoyed. They are not very amusing even as pornography.[7]

Lermontov gained popularity, however, through his poetic skills. The cadets produced a school magazine, *Shkolnaya zarya* [School Dawn], which was copied by hand. Some of Lermontov's poems appeared here signed "Mayoshka," a nickname given him by his friends which he happily accepted. It is a Russified version of "Mayeux," a figure in contemporary French caricatures known for his witticisms and caustic jokes. There is no doubt that Lermontov had a sharp tongue, but he also generally accepted in good humor remarks aimed at him. Unfortunately, certain fellow cadets were not so understanding, and he continually made enemies when he failed to check his tongue.

Almost immediately upon entering the Cavalry School Lermontov had a severe accident, after which it took him two months to recuperate. He had tried to show off by riding a horse that had not been fully broken, and lost control of it. In a melee with another horse, he cut his right leg just below the knee. It was not set properly, so that thereafter he walked with a slight limp and a bowed leg. His model Byron limped too, having been born with a club foot.

As an officer later on, Lermontov spared no expense to own the best horses. He kept several, in part because he liked to ride frequently from his quarters at the Imperial Summer Palace of Tsarskoe Selo to visit friends in St. Petersburg. A splendid horse then was the equivalent of today's fast car.

His wenching and drinking soon changed him a great deal. On 4 August 1833, Lermontov wrote to Maria Lopukhina:

The time of my dreams has passed; the time for believing is long gone; now I want material pleasures, happiness that I can touch, happiness that can be bought with gold, that one can carry in one's pocket like a snuff-box, happiness that beguiles only my senses while leaving my soul in peace and quiet! That is what I want now. As you can see, dear friend, I have changed somewhat since we last met. When I saw my beautiful dreams vanish, I told myself that it simply was not worth creating new ones. I thought it better to try to get along without them. (4:381)

This may sound like a letter home from a worldly-wise college freshman (Lermontov was only eighteen at the time), but still he had matured rapidly.

It should be noted that reading literature and writing poetry (except for bawdy verses) were considered the equivalent of "conduct unbecoming an officer and a gentleman" at the Cavalry School. And yet Lermontov did continue to read and write serious works, if much less intensively than in Moscow. He concealed this side of his life from the authorities and his fellow cadets alike. Alexander Merinsky was one of the few who ever witnessed it:

In the evenings after class our poet would often make for some distant empty classroom, trying not to attract the attention of any of his friends. There he would sit alone for a long time writing until the early hours of the morning. Sometimes he would draw. He drew quite well and loved to sketch views of the Caucasus and Circassians galloping along mountain trails. (*Vosp.*, 128)

Merinsky remarks that Lermontov was very reluctant to allow anyone even to read his serious poems, let alone copy them.

The Social Round

But if Lermontov had his serious occupations which he kept hidden, he also enjoyed to the full the joys of being an officer, which he became on 22 November 1834, after two years of military training. That very evening he attended a ball in his resplendent new uniform, which his grandmother already had made. Mme Arsenieva also had a portrait done of him in this uniform. Like the other portraits of Lermontov, it makes him look a great deal more dashing than he apparently did in real life to his contemporaries.

In a letter to Maria Lopukhina of 23 December 1834, Lermontov describes his new social aplomb:

I am beginning to move into society now in order to make myself known, and to prove that I am capable of finding pleasure in good company. Ah! I am paying court to young ladies, and at the end of a declaration of love I make risque remarks. It still amuses me a little, and although there is nothing particularly new about all this, it is not that common. (4:385–86)

An immediate victim of Lermontov's new prowess was Ekaterina Sushkova, the same young lady who had treated him as a boy four years previously. Now when Lermontov courted her again, she responded, no doubt thinking that he would not make a bad match. He merely wished, however, to make a name for himself in society as a cavalier. With cold calculation, like one of his own heroes, Lermontov set out to compromise her while leaving himself in the clear, free to boast of his exploits. And he did that in a letter to Sashenka Vereshchagina written in the spring of 1835, after the dust had settled, when he recounted the whole story quite shamelessly. When they were alone, he behaved like an adoring swain, but in public Lermontov treated Sushkova rather distantly. She endured this public humiliation for some time before realizing that Lermontov was using her to impress his friends. Then he delivered the coup de grace by sending Sushkova an anonymous four-page letter warning her against the machinations of "M. L.," and thereafter he was no longer a welcome guest at Sushkova's home. On the same day Sushkova received the anonymous letter (5 January 1835), Aleksey Lopukhin left St. Petersburg. He had courted Sushkova before Lermontov's interruption: no doubt Lermontov also hoped to prevent a possible marriage between Aleksey and Sushkova, whom he regarded as unworthy of his friend.

As Lermontov put it in his letter to Sashenka, "Now I do not write novels—I live them" (4:391). But at that moment of triumph, Lopukhin's sister Varvara struck Lermontov a blow by marrying a man fifteen years her senior. At the end of his long letter to 'Sashenka Vereshchagina, Lermontov commented on Varvara's impending marriage (it took place on 25 May): "I hope she lives in conjugal bliss until her silver wedding anniversary."

In fact, however, though Lermontov had not seen Varvara for two and a half years, he took the news very hard. The two must have corresponded, but her husband destroyed the letters after the marriage. Lermontov viewed Varvara as an ideal, the "angel" to his "demon." Thus she appears in many of his works, including *A Hero of Our Time,* where she is presented in her last incarnation as Vera, Pechorin's secret love.

Literary Notoriety

It was in early 1837 that the young social lion burst upon the literary scene. The occasion was the wounding of Alexander Pushkin in a pistol duel and his subsequent death on 29 January. Lermontov responded to this tragedy with a poetic piece of fiery indignation, "Smert poeta" [Death of a Poet], which was widely circulated in manuscript, largely through the efforts of his close friend Svyatoslav Raevsky. Perhaps Lermontov did not realize the impact his rhetoric would have upon the reading public, but if so he soon realized that the poem was likely to bring the wrath of the authorities upon him.

Though he knew that his grandmother could enlist the assistance of highly placed relatives and friends, he himself made a point of calling on his friend Andrey Muravyov to ask for his assistance, but to no avail in the end. In his memoirs Muravyov claims that the original version of the poem—before Lermontov added a concluding sixteen-line portion attacking the court—had many admirers in high places and was not perceived as even seditious, let alone worthy of prosecution (*Vosp.*, 196). General Alexander Benckendorff, head of the secret police, who avoided trouble whenever possible, wanted to keep the whole matter quiet. But Anna Khitrovo, daughter of General Mikhail Kutuzov, the hero of the Napoleonic campaigns, made a great issue of the poem's last sixteen lines, demanding that some action be taken to defend the honor of the court and high society. Benckendorff had no choice but to report fully on the matter to Nicholas I, who decided that young Lermontov would have to be dealt with firmly.

On or about 18 February, Lermontov was arrested for questioning, and his apartment was searched on 20 February. Raevsky was also arrested and his apartment searched. To be blunt about it, Lermontov behaved poorly in his first brush with Benckendorff's gendarmes. In his formal written statement, a repentant and apologetic one, Lermontov told the interrogators that Raevsky had asked to copy the poem and then to distribute it, suggesting that this was done without his permission.[8]

Raevsky, for his part, did all he could to present Lermontov in a favorable light (*Vosp.*, 389–92). He pointed out that Lermontov had openly signed his name to the poem; the censorship could have stopped the poem if it found it offensive. He also stressed that they both felt it permissible to attack the enemies of Pushkin, a great Russian poet who had received favors in the past from the Tsar.

After being held for a short time, Lermontov was officially sentenced on 27 February. He was transferred without loss of rank to the Nizhegorodsky Dragoons in the Caucasus.

Raevsky, who was poor and suffered from rheumatism, received a harsher penalty than Lermontov. He was sent to serve as a "provincial secretary" (a very low rank) at the pleasure of the governor in the northern town of Olonets, located near what is now the border with Finland.

The two sentences were announced on the day Lermontov was released from detention. He was allowed to say goodbye to his family, and he immediately wrote to Raevsky to explain his behavior. Lermontov said he was deeply distressed to learn that he had been the cause of Raevsky's troubles. He had only implicated his friend when threatened with reduction to the ranks, and then after he had been assured that nothing would happen to Raevsky:

I remembered my grandmother . . . I just could not . . . I sacrificed you for her sake. . . . What I felt at that moment, I cannot say, but I am sure that you will understand me and forgive me and still consider me worthy of your friendship. (4:399)

Lermontov's performance was not very edifying, most would agree. Here is the Byronic man-about-town, the creator of uncompromising, steely-eyed rebels, folding under interrogation. To his credit, though, he realized at once how badly he had betrayed his friend. Raevsky seems to have been very understanding, much to Lermontov's relief.

Raevsky also suffered more than his well-connected friend. Lermontov, still an officer, began his leisurely journey to the south on 19 March, arriving four days later in Moscow, where he lingered until 10 April. Having then caught cold on the way, Lermontov halted in Stavropol in early May to take the waters. Indeed, he seems to have spent the whole period of his exile either in Stavropol or traveling from one interesting spot to another, always with the help of friends or relatives.

In the meantime, Mme Arsenieva had found a willing ally in Benckendorff, who twice wrote to Nicholas suggesting that Lermontov be forgiven. The Tsar visited the Caucasus on an inspection tour in October, and was pleased with the state of the troops he saw, including Lermontov's own regiment (though

Lermontov was absent on his travels at the time). On 11 October, in the Georgian capital of Tbilisi, Lermontov was ordered to report to the Grodnensky Hussar Regiment, then stationed in the Province of Novgorod (*Letopis,* 85). This was short of a pardon, but still a favorable action since Novgorod is located some 100 miles south of St. Petersburg.

But Lermontov was in no hurry to take up his new assignment. He did not even start out until December, and then spent most of January in Moscow before reporting finally to his regiment on 27 February 1838. Even then Lermontov continued to live an easy life, visiting the capital at least twice before being officially pardoned on 9 April and allowed to return permanently to the Life Guard Hussars at Tsarskoe Selo. Exile in those days, if one had the right connections, was not too painful.

All this time Raevsky stayed in the miserable town of Olonets. He was not pardoned until 19 December 1838 and did not return to St. Petersburg until early April 1839, one year after Lermontov, and more than two years after their troubles had started. Within hours of his arrival, Lermontov rushed to see him. Raevsky's young sister recalled the scene as Lermontov entered the room, embraced Raevsky, and repeated with tears in his eyes: "Forgive me, forgive me, dear friend!" (*Letopis,* 101). And Raevsky did forgive Lermontov.

The Capital and Exile

Lermontov's production of lyrics fell during 1838–39, a second St. Petersburg period. Somehow the capital never provided him a creative environment for lyric poetry. Lermontov wrote a great many other things in these two years, however, mostly narrative poems and prose fiction. His lyrical impulse revived once more only at the beginning of 1840, when he was exiled again to the Caucasus.

During the two years Lermontov spent in St. Petersburg he led a dual existence. On the one hand, he lived the life of a Hussar social lion, attending parties, the theater, and magnificent balls at the palaces of Tsarskoe Selo and Pavlovsk. On the other hand, he continued to lead an intellectual existence quite apart from the superficial glitter of St. Petersburg high society. Lermontov's two worlds met only in his poems castigating the hollowness and malice of this society.

·Now, for the first time, Lermontov became a visible participant in the cultural life of his time. "Death of a Poet" had brought him to the attention of the major authors of the day. In a letter of 15 February 1838, written during a visit to St. Petersburg, he tells Maria Lopukhina that Vasily Zhukovsky had asked to see his narrative poem *The Tambov Treasurer's Wife* and had read it together with Peter Vyazemsky: "They liked it a lot, and it will appear in the next issue of *Sovremennik* [The Contemporary]" (4:406). Prince Vyazemsky had been a close personal friend of Pushkin's; Zhukovsky, the doyen of Russian poetry, was very well connected at court (he tutored the future Tsar Alexander II).

Lermontov's friend Svyatoslav Raevsky helped build his growing public reputation as a poet. Raevsky introduced Lermontov to Andrey Kraevsky, the editor of a new and important journal that began publication in early 1839. Thereafter Lermontov's poems appeared regularly in *Otechestvennye zapiski* [Notes of the Fatherland].

One of Lermontov's important poems, in fact, appeared in the very first issue of *Otechestvennye zapiski* in January 1839. "Duma" [Meditation] opens with the lines:

> Sadly I look upon our generation!
> Its future is either empty or dark;
> Meanwhile, under the burden of knowledge and doubt,
> It grows old in idleness.

In its entirety "Meditation" represents a sophisticated development of themes articulated earlier, but at the same time it looks forward to Lermontov's dissection of his generation's brilliant scion, Grigory Pechorin (*A Hero of Our Time*), who is certainly "shamefully indifferent to both good and evil," as Lermontov phrases it here. Lermontov ends his poem with a prophecy that future generations will dismiss his own with a "bitter smile of disdain."

At this time Lermontov made a valuable new acquaintance in Ekaterina Karamzina, widow of the famous writer and historian Nikolay Karamzin. Mme Karamzina and her daughter Sophia maintained a literary salon where Lermontov met numerous interesting people in the cultural world of the capital. In the summer Lermontov visited the Karamzin countryhouse near Tsarskoe Selo almost every day, and the rest of the year he visited the Karamzin apartment in St. Petersburg almost as frequently.

In the Karamzin home Lermontov could discuss his poetry in congenial surroundings, in addition to participating in charades, games, masquerades, and amateur theatricals.

Lermontov was of course delighted by his notoriety in St. Petersburg society. He continued to behave disdainfully with those who bored him and to exercise his wit at others' expense. He had little regard for his military obligations. In September 1838 he once turned up on parade with a toy sword, and was put in the guardhouse for three weeks. This did not dismay him: he later appeared on parade with an enormously long sword that dragged on the ground.

Indeed Lermontov wanted to resign from the cavalry, but Mme Arsenieva opposed any such move, perhaps still hoping for an illustrious military career for him. At the end of 1838 Lermontov wrote to Maria Lopukhina that he had requested a leave of absence first for a year, then a month, then two weeks. He was turned down by the Grand Duke, his commander, who was thoroughly weary of Lermontov's antics. He was not even permitted to return to the Caucasus: "They won't even let me get killed," he complained. Lermontov then speaks of his love-hate relationship with St. Petersburg high society:

Perhaps it seems strange to you that I should seek pleasures in order to be bored and go the rounds of the salons when there is nothing interesting in them. Well, I will tell you why I do it. You know that my greatest fault is vanity and pride. There was a time when I tried to enter this society as a novice, and I was refused admittance; the doors of the aristocracy were closed to me. Now I enter this same society no longer as a petitioner, but as a man who has won his right to be there. (4:412)

Lermontov revealed more of himself to Maria Lopukhina than he had to anyone else. As we read this letter we feel we are reading an intimate journal, and Lermontov did ask Maria not to reveal what he had said to anyone. He added that society disgusted him, and swore to avenge himself against it if he should become a target of its calumny.

Lermontov's vengeance took the forms of occasional outbursts of raffish behavior and poetic attacks. But Lermontov and official St. Petersburg were on a collision course. Even his promotion from cornet to lieutenant, announced on 6 December 1839, failed to placate him. He seemed determined to provoke the authorities in some fashion.

He succeeded early in 1840. His relationship with high society was beginning to irritate him. Its malicious gossip repelled him, and he quite likely realized that society appealed to the darker side of his nature. The future novelist Ivan Turgenev recalled seeing Lermontov in late December at a private home:

There was in Lermontov's appearance something ominous and tragic; his dark complexion and large, somber, motionless eyes conveyed a sense of gloomy, evil power and pensive scorn and passion. There was a strange discord between his severe gaze and the expression of his almost childishly tender, protruding lips. (*Letopis,* 110–11)

A few days later Turgenev saw Lermontov again, this time at a New Year's Eve masquerade ball held at the Assembly Hall of the Nobility. Lermontov was surrounded by masked ladies who twittered about him, giving him no peace as, deep in thought, he tried to ignore them.

At this ball Lermontov committed the first of three acts which turned both the authorities and society against him more seriously than ever before. He made insulting remarks to two of Tsar Nicholas's daughters, who were dressed as pink and blue dominoes but whose identity was known to everyone. Exactly what he said is not known, but the Tsar's daughter Maria was angry enough to encourage another author to write a story lampooning Lermontov as a social climber.

Lermontov's second offense was the publication in the January issue of *Otechestvennye zapiski* of a scathing attack on St. Petersburg high society in a poem "1-go yanvarya" [January 1], which begins "How often, surrounded by a motley crowd." The work opens with harsh comments on the pretenses and "casual brazenness of city beauties." In the central stanzas, however, the poet recalls the childhood joys of country living, the "holy sounds of years dead and gone." Inevitably, in the final stanza the poet compares his daydream to "an uninvited guest at a party" as he returns to reality. But the closing three lines probably aroused the most hostility in high society:

> Oh, how I want to shame their gaiety
> And boldly hurl in their faces my iron verses
> Forged with bitterness and hatred! . . .

Lermontov's third act of defiance was a duel with Ernest de Barante, son of the French ambassador. No one knows what caused the dispute between them at a ball.

De Barante challenged Lermontov, and as the "injured party" selected rapiers for weapons. The duel occurred two days later at noon, in a wet snowfall. The two men staggered about knee-deep in snow for about ten minutes until Lermontov was slightly wounded in the forearm. Then the combatants turned to pistols. De Barante's gun misfired, Lermontov shot into the air, and the two men shook hands and parted (*Letopis,* 115–16).

Word of the duel spread quickly. As by that time dueling was forbidden, Lermontov had to supply a written explanation. It is beautifully composed, without apologies or any attempt at self-justification. Instead of saying that he had fired into the air rather than shoot at the defenseless Frenchman, Lermontov wrote that he "was a little late in firing." He was arrested and detained on 10 March, while a commission of inquiry was appointed.

On 15 March the critic Vissarion Belinsky wrote to a friend in Moscow that the Tsar had remarked that since Lermontov had dueled with a Frenchman rather than a Russian, "three quarters of the guilt can be forgotten." In fact, it seems very likely that Lermontov would have been sentenced to only six months or so in the infantry at the same rank before being allowed to return to the Life Guard Hussars. Lermontov, however, heard a rumor that de Barante had denied that he (Lermontov) had deliberately fired into the air. He called the Frenchman in and suggested they fight again. De Barante prudently refused and left Russia for Paris the next day.

Friends and relatives alike condemned Lermontov's behavior: for one thing, receiving a visitor while under arrest was strictly forbidden. Instead of being let off lightly, Lermontov was ordered on 13 April 1840 to report to the Tenginsky Infantry Regiment in the Caucasus, though he retained his rank as a lieutenant. Mme Arsenieva could no longer persuade Benckendorff to intercede on his behalf. In fact, Benckendorff tried to force Lermontov to write a letter of apology to de Barante, but apparently Nicholas told Benckendorff to drop the idea.

After his case was settled, Lermontov could receive visitors. One was Belinsky, who reported to a friend that they had a lively conversation about the novels of Sir Walter Scott, whom Lermontov thought "dry," and James Fenimore Cooper, whose work he felt contained much more "poetry." Lermontov left St. Petersburg for the Caucasus in early May.

Death of a Poet

Lermontov began his second exile as he had begun his first: with a leisurely journey that included a stay of three weeks in Moscow. There he visited many friends, old and new, and attended a name-day celebration for Nikolay Gogol, where he read a section from *The Novice*. He also visited the future Slavophile Yury Samarin, with whom he became fast friends. He searched out Samarin the following year, when traveling to and from the Caucasus, for further long discussions. As he showed Samarin his sketches and described the suffering of men in battle, he nearly burst into tears. Samarin says that Lermontov was ashamed of revealing his feelings and tried to explain away his emotionalism as the result of strained nerves (*Vosp.*, 297).

Lermontov left Moscow at the end of May, arriving on 10 June in Stavropol, where he reported to General Pavel Grabbe, commander of the Russian forces in the region. Lermontov persuaded General Grabbe to ignore his assignment to the Tenginsky Regiment and instead send him with Russian forces attempting to capture the prophet-warrior Shamyl, who continued to give the Russians great problems for many years. Lermontov's objective in ignoring official orders was to see as much action as possible in the hope of distinguishing himself and thus obtaining an early pardon: this was standard practice for exiled officers at that time.

Lermontov certainly saw action. He displayed great courage in hand-to-hand battles on several occasions, particularly at the Valerik River on 11 July. He sketched scenes from that battle, and also wrote a remarkable poem about it beginning "Ya k vam pishu sluchàyno . . ." ("I am writing to you by chance . . .") (1:451–52). The poem is particularly noteworthy for its sustained tone and natural ease of expression. Gone is the melodrama of his earlier poems. For a brief moment after the terrible bloodletting the writer looks up at the beautiful mountains in the distance:

> And with a secret and heartfelt sadness
> I thought: pathetic man.
> What does he want! . . . the sky is clear;
> Beneath the sky there is plenty of room for all,
> But constantly and vainly
> He alone is at war—for what?

In the meantime, back in St. Petersburg, Mme Arsenieva was still lobbying on behalf of her grandson. On 11 December 1840, Minister of War Alexander Chernyshyov announced that the Tsar had graciously granted Mme Arsenieva's petition and Lermontov would be allowed to return for two months' leave to see her, since she claimed that she was deathly ill.

On 24 December Colonel Prince Golitsyn, commander of cavalry on the left flank of the Cossack Line, recommended to General Grabbe that Lermontov be awarded a gold saber inscribed "For Courage." On 14 January Lermontov received the promised two-month pass and left immediately for St. Petersburg. He arrived on 5 February and attended a ball that same evening before reporting to his commanding officer. This typically foolhardy act horrified his friends and well-wishers: after receiving a leave to see his sick grandmother, Lermontov had rushed to a ball when he was still officially in disfavor. In his memoirs Vladimir Sollogub recalls how angry he was with Lermontov:

"What on earth are you doing here!" I shouted at him. "Get out of here, Lermontov, or you'll be arrested! See how sternly Grand Duke Mikhail Pavlovich is staring at you!" (*Vosp.*, 269)

Lermontov declined to leave, and this act of brazen disrespect very likely cost him the commendations and the gold saber that should have been his. With one idiotic gesture he had antagonized the authorities and undermined all Mme Arsenieva's achievements over the preceding several months. Furthermore, the recommendations for medals and honors made the authorities realize that Lermontov was fighting in engagements instead of reporting as assigned. Belated attempts were made to have him report according to orders in the summer of 1841, but by then Lermontov was already dead.

According to Countess Evdokiya Rostopchina, with whom Lermontov became close friends at the time, the late winter and early spring of 1841 were one of the happiest times of his life.[9] In rare good humor, he attended many social functions with his old friends, including the Karamzins. Apparently the authorities had no intention of curtailing his leave, and in fact granted him an additional month. He tried to prolong his stay, and also to obtain permission to retire from military service, but was refused.

For a long time Mme Arsenieva was the chief obstacle to his retirement. When she did finally ask Benckendorff, he refused— not surprisingly, since he detested Lermontov. That personal dislike, however, does not mean that Lermontov was hounded to his death by Tsar Nicholas I or Count Benckendorff or anyone else in authority. On the contrary, in view of the fact that he continually antagonized them, the authorities treated Lermontov with reasonable fairness. He was, after all, living in a society where people were not free to conduct their lives as they wished.[10]

When it was discovered that Lermontov had stayed in St. Petersburg beyond his official leave, he was ordered to depart within 48 hours. He left on 14 April. Once again he made a leisurely journey south, stopping in Moscow for a week. Once again he contracted a convenient illness and obtained permission to take the waters at Pyatigorsk. There he rented a house with his old friend "Mongo" Stolypin. They had a most enjoyable time at Pyatigorsk, visiting homes, arranging picnics, and riding about the spectacular countryside.

Lermontov might have remained in Pyatigorsk for the whole summer, as he had in his first exile of 1837, had he not made caustic remarks at the expense of Nikolay Martynov, a retired major whom Lermontov had known for years. Lermontov continually taunted Martynov about his exaggerated native dress and made him look ridiculous in front of young ladies he wished to impress. As so often, Lermontov was immediately sorry after the damage was done, and clearly thought the whole matter would subside. Lermontov never understood the impact of his behavior on other people. He childishly thought that if he changed, the other person should respond in kind. But Martynov was adamant, and a duel took place on 15 July just outside town in an eerie replay of the duel in *A Hero of Our Time*.

Lermontov was in an excellent mood on his way to the duel. He spoke to a friend about plans to write a trilogy of historical novels and other projects. Then, just as in his first duel, Lermontov made no attempt to fire. Martynov, however, advanced deliberately and rapidly to the marker and shot Lermontov in the heart, killing him instantly.

Despite the claims of certain Soviet scholars, there is absolutely no evidence that the duel was the culmination of a conspiracy headed by the Tsar to do away with Lermontov.[11] It was the culmination, if anything, of a long-standing animosity between Lermontov and the Martynov family. We recall that at a New Year's party nine years before, Lermontov wrote a "horoscope" for one of Martynov's young sisters which was much more biting than any other piece he composed on that occasion. During his first exile Lermontov had been given a packet of letters containing

300 rubles by the Martynov family for transmission to Nikolay Martynov. Lermontov lost it, along with most of his luggage, during his travels, and gave Martynov 300 rubles of his own money instead. Martynov's mother had written to Nikolay that she suspected Lermontov had opened the packet, read the letters, and taken the money himself (*Letopis,* 87). This groundless suspicion illustrates the bad feeling between the family and Lermontov. Then, in 1840, on his way to his second exile, Lermontov again stopped in Moscow and reportedly was too attentive to the Martynov sisters to suit their parents. Martynov was informed about Lermontov's behavior. All these things suggest that Martynov did not care for Lermontov even before the incident at Pyatigorsk in July 1841.

All along, Lermontov's sharp tongue had made him many enemies, though he could be a delightful companion when he wished. In his memoirs the writer Ivan Panaev reports that many of Lermontov's schoolmates and fellow officers disliked him as a cliquish sort. He also had a nasty habit of discovering a person's comic side and then constantly harping on it:

"It is strange," one of his comrades told me. "In essence he was, if you wish, a nice fellow: he was ready to have fun, go out on the town just like anyone else. But he did not have an ounce of good nature in his body. He always had to have a victim; without one he could not be comfortable. Once he had chosen a victim, he pursued him without mercy. He was bound to end up tragically as he did: if it hadn't been Martynov, somebody else would have killed him." (*Vosp.,* 233)

That is certainly a damning indictment. Unfortunately, there is much evidence to support it, including the events leading up to the duel with Martynov.[12]

Of course that is not the whole story. One could find just as many memoirists who praise Lermontov and recall his charm and warmth. We may recall his touching letter to Aleksey Lopukhin in which he congratulated him on a new son and enclosed the poem beginning "The birth of a sweet baby." In his letter Lermontov says in part:

You have achieved your goal, but I never will. I'll just sit in some hole, and that is the last anyone will hear of me. Maybe they will pray for me. I am like a man who tried to taste all the dishes at once, but got indigestion before eating his fill; then had to get rid of the indigestion, incidentally, by writing poetry. (1:415)

Here is Lermontov with his defenses down, a vulnerable young man who senses that life may be passing him by. [13]

Lermontov was so changeable that he could make very different impressions on the same person over a short time. For example, Belinsky disliked Lermontov the first time they met but found him charming after a second encounter. Exactly the same thing happened to the young German poet Friedrich Bodenstedt, who met Lermontov on two successive evenings in Moscow in 1841. On the first occasion Lermontov mocked someone else at the table for so long that the "victim" finally took offense. The next evening Lermontov was charming and gave an entirely different impression (*Vosp.*, 289–91).

In the case of his final duel, though, as far as we can tell, Lermontov was entirely at fault, for he provoked Martynov beyond endurance. Martynov was a rather flashy, self-important fellow, and Lermontov should have had the wit not to torment such a mediocrity. And at the duel itself Lermontov reportedly declared that he had no intention of "firing at that fool." If Martynov had not intended to shoot already, that comment must have tipped the scales of tragedy. [14]

Chapter Two

"No, I Am Not Byron . . .": The Moscow Period (1828–32)

The Byronic Hero

Lord Byron was the dominant cultural and social figure of his time, the equivalent in civilian clothes of Napoleon Bonaparte, who dominated most of Europe until his defeat in 1815 at Waterloo. Although Napoleon had been a major foe of the British, Byron very much admired him, and was instrumental in creating the cult of Napoleon as a titanic figure brought low by the fates and lesser men. In his narrative poem *Childe Harold's Pilgrimage* Byron included the following stanza on Napoleon after his downfall:

> Yet well thy soul hath brooked the turning tide
> With that untaught innate philosophy,
> Which, be it wisdom, coldness, or deep pride,
> Is gall and wormwood to an enemy.
> When the whole host of hatred stood hard by
> To watch and mock thee shrinking, thou hast smiled
> With a sedate and all-enduring eye;—
> When fortune fled her spoiled and favorite child,
> He stood unbowed beneath the ills upon him piled.
>
> (Canto III, 343–51)

Here Napoleon appears as a "Byronic hero," the English poet's chief contribution to the culture of the first half of the nineteenth century. Byron was himself the leading exemplar of the type, which he described in such works as *Childe Harold, Cain,* and *Manfred.*

The origins of the Byronic hero—the demonic, long-suffering, but proud and rebellious loner—are to be found in the Romantic view of Satan in Milton's *Paradise Lost,* in the so-called Gothic novels of the late eighteenth and early nineteenth centuries in England, and in the works of the French writers François Chateaubriand and Benjamin Constant. But it was Byron who popularized the type, who indeed lived the role himself, traveling across Europe after becoming a social outcast in England because of his outrageous behavior, which included an affair with his half-sister.

The central characteristics of the Byronic hero have been succinctly summarized by David Perkins:

He is a man greater than others in emotion, capability, and suffering. Only among wild and vast forms of nature—the ocean, the precipices and glaciers of the Alps—can he find a counterpart to his own titanic passions. Driven by a demon within, he is fatal to himself and others; for no one can resist his hypnotic fascination and authority. He has committed a sin that itself expresses his superiority: lesser men could not even conceive a like transgression. Against his own suffering he brings to bear a superhuman pride and fortitude. Indeed, without the horror of his fate there could not be the splendor of self-assertion and self-mastery in which he experiences a strange joy and triumph. [1]

The appeal of the Byronic hero—not simply as a literary persona but as a social model—was quite extraordinary throughout Europe.

Byron's influence reached Russia very early, even before his death in 1824, through the medium of French translations. Though Lermontov first became familiar with Byron in French translations, he studied English and later read him in the original. [2]

Alexander Pushkin (1799–1837), the most famous poet in the Russian language and the founder of Russian literature, became

Lermontov's first literary mentor. Pushkin provided Lermontov a poetic example, and also introduced Lermontov to the Byronic hero and the "Byronic poem."

With Pushkin Russian poetry became "elegiac" in the sense that it focused its attention on the intimate feelings of the poet, or of his lyrical hero. And Lermontov became the most Romantic of the Russian poets. To a far greater extent than Pushkin, Lermontov infused the elegiac impulse into everything he wrote. He is also the most "Byronic" of the Russian poets in that his works constitute an extended exploration of his own personality. The Romantic poet is involved in his own personal drama and devotes his poems to a close analysis of his own feelings, often excluding the emotions of other people and the objective world.

The Earliest Writings

Lermontov's juvenilia of the Moscow period—most of which remained unknown to his contemporaries and were never intended for publication—consist of sixteen narrative poems (some incomplete), three plays (one in verse), and nearly 300 lyrics or short poems (including epigrams, album verses, translations, and adaptations). This is an extraordinary output for one so young, although Lermontov did borrow occasional lines from other poets and repeatedly cannibalized his own poems when creating new ones. He continued this latter habit throughout his lifetime, keeping fair copies of his works in notebooks which have survived, returning to them from time to time to cross sections out, change lines, or transfer them from one work to another.[3]

The notebooks constitute simultaneously a poetic workshop and a personal journal, in which Lermontov put into verse his experiences, his feelings of anger and frustration, his dreams, and his thoughts. That he was quite well aware of the notebooks' latter function is shown by a passage from his play *Stranny chelovek* [The Strange Man], written in 1831. After the death of the hero, Vladimir Arbenin, an autobiographical figure, one of the guests at a party mentions that Arbenin's private papers have been examined:

They found many notebooks in his room, which contain everything that was in his heart; there is both prose and verse, full of deep thoughts and fiery emotions! I am sure that if his passions had not destroyed him so soon, then he might have become one of our best writers. One can see genius in these early efforts! (3:255)

Such self-congratulation is perhaps excusable in one so young. After all, these early works were for his eyes only, and Lermontov did indeed become one of Russia's greatest poets. Later generations, however, have not shared his high opinion of these "early efforts." In fact, Lermontov's friends and admirers, beginning with Akim Shan-Girey (*Vosp.*, 36), regretted that the vast majority of them ever saw the light of day.

Nearly all Lermontov's early works are heavily autobiographical, but they also borrow extensively from the authors he most admired: first Pushkin, then Schiller (especially in the plays), and—most important—Byron. Following the suggestions of Boris Eykhenbaum, we may detect several major themes running through all the juvenilia: (1) the tragic nature of love; (2) the cult of Napoleon; (3) demonism—one is fated to destroy what one loves; (4) disillusionment; (5) vengeance; (6) a passion for freedom, both personal and social; and (7) "original innocence"— life on earth is a fall from some pure existence in the past.[4] As we shall see, these are themes of central importance in Lermontov's more mature works also. Though they have little literary merit, the works of the Moscow period tell us much about Lermontov as a person, and about his poetic preferences.

Narrative Poems

In one of his autobiographical notes of 1830, Lermontov recalled that he began to "scribble verses" *(marat stikhi)* in 1828. His first effort was a narrative poem entitled *Cherkesy* [The Circassians], written the summer before he returned to Moscow to enter the School for the Nobility.[5] Its melodramatic style and exotic Caucasian setting recall Pushkin's so-called Southern Poems written during his exile from 1820 to 1824. In his turn, Pushkin had learned to write this type of narrative poem from

Byron. Lermontov was very familiar with both Pushkin and Byron at least by 1827, for in a notebook of that year he copied out both Pushkin's "Bakhchisaraysky fontan" [The Fountain of Bakhchisaray] and Byron's "The Prisoner of Chillon" in a beautiful Russian translation by Vasily Zhukovsky (1783–1852).

Lermontov visited the Caucasus twice as a child, with the second visit taking place in 1825. His personal impressions of the magnificent mountains there must have intensified his response to the exotic tales in verse that he was reading and imitating. Furthermore, Russia was constantly at war in the border region with the native tribes, who provided Lermontov with ready-made Romantic heroes and villains in an atmosphere of intrigue and bravado.

It is not surprising that Lermontov began his literary career with narrative poems, or tales in verse, as they were often called. The "Byronic epic" was one of the most popular Romantic genres; it provided the main vehicle for the "Byronic hero." Byron created this vehicle by making significant changes in the traditional epic poems that neoclassicists of the seventeenth and eighteenth centuries had put at the top of their hierarchy of genres. He replaced the pseudo-historical or mythical national epics with verse tales about fictional characters set in contemporary times, even if the settings were exotic.

The Romantic poets rejoiced in the freedom of this new style of poem. They ostentatiously violated the many rules and regulations that tradition had established. For example, in the earlier verse epics the narrator stayed in the background and narrated in a solemn, objective manner, while the Romantic poet went out of his way to intrude into the action, to comment on both character and event, and to interrupt the flow of the narration with random digressions on his personal opinions and feelings. The emotional and moral tone of narrative poetry changed completely. Passion replaced duty as an ideal while the ecstasy and torments of love supplanted the triumph of victory and the agony of defeat on the battlefield.

Several Russian writers tried their hand at the new type of Byronic narrative poem, but only Pushkin and his successor Ler-

montov were successful. During the greater part of Pushkin's
four-year exile in the South, which began in 1820, he was under
the influence of Byron. The influence was never total, however;
it was merely a phase in Pushkin's protean career and passed
much more quickly than did Lermontov's fascination with Byron
and Byronism. We must remember, though, that Lermontov was
only twelve or thirteen when captivated by Byron; Pushkin came
to Byron when he was twenty, after cutting his poetic teeth on
eighteenth-century French wit and elegance.

The very titles of Lermontov's early narrative poems show the
influence of Pushkin and Byron: *The Circassians, A Captive in the
Caucasus, The Corsair*. Many of the poems, in addition, have
English epigraphs taken from Byron's works. The time and place
in which the poems are set vary quite considerably; they move
from the Caucasus to Scandinavia and ancient Russia and to Spain
and Italy. Lermontov also tried his hand at portraying the "fallen
angel," following the example of Byron's *Cain* and *Heaven and
Earth*. His most famous effort of this sort was *Demon* [The De-
mon], which he began in 1829 and continued to revise and rework
for ten years.

This apparent variety is deceptive, however. The central figure
of the Byronic hero dominates all the poems, and the narration
consists almost exclusively of extended monologue, in which the
hero-narrator protests against his fate and vows vengeance for
some real or imagined wrong. The poems are full of passion,
jealousy, betrayal, and the vain search for freedom.

The poems are also autobiographical in the sense that the heroes
represent projections of Lermontov's personality. There is much
posturing in the flashing eyes, strong wills, avenging of affronts
and betrayals, and the easy handling of beautiful women to be
found in them. Lermontov was much too close to his heroes, and
so they remain idealized, one-sided figments of his imagination.
Lermontov still lacked the artistic skill to write persuasively about
things he had never experienced.

If there is a difference between Lermontov's poems and Byron's,
it is that Lermontov's heroes are more dynamic and active, his
poems more violent and narrated on a more strident, less elegiac

level. In other words, he is more extreme than Byron, "plus royaliste que le roi même."

Several of his poems of this period are unfinished. Why did Lermontov stop and start so frequently? Certainly not because he lacked the desire or will to complete a project once begun. The answer is probably that, young though he was, Lermontov could sense that something was wrong. Dissatisfied with what he wrote, he kept trying new settings, new periods, new situations. At this stage, Lermontov was convinced that the narrative poem was the vehicle he needed; it was only later that he moved away from the narrative poem to prose fiction as a more suitable medium.

The Plays

Not until the summer of 1830 did Lermontov begin his first play, but it was inevitable that he would turn his attention to drama sooner or later. He had enjoyed the theater and opera since childhood. In fact, he had once begun, but then dropped, a libretto based on Pushkin's poem *The Gypsies.* He displayed unusual skill in making puppet figures from wax, and loved putting on puppet shows and participating in amateur theatricals.

Lermontov's typically Romantic enthusiasm for Shakespeare is clear from a letter he wrote in February 1830 to his aunt, Maria Shan-Girey. He defends Shakespeare, declaring that *Hamlet* is the most obvious demonstration of his greatness and quoting some dialogue which he had evidently translated himself (4:360–62). The previous year Lermontov had translated (incorrectly) part of the German reworking of *Macbeth* by Friedrich Schiller, who was far more important than Shakespeare for Lermontov as a dramatist.

To be more precise, Lermontov was interested in the young Schiller of the *Sturm und Drang* (Storm and Stress) period rather than the "Classical" Schiller, with his notions of the "beautiful soul" and universal freedom. Schiller's later plays did not have nearly the same impact on Lermontov as did the early melodramas *Die Räuber* [The Robbers, 1781] and *Kabale und Liebe* [Intrigue and Love, 1783], both of which he saw on the Moscow stage. In Schiller's transitional play, *Don Carlos* (1787), which marks

his shift to Classicism, Lermontov paid much more attention to
the first part, dealing with Don Carlos's hatred for his father,
Phillip II, than to the second half, where the personal conflict
yields to the more general problem of freedom and dignity for
all men.

In his plays as in his narrative poems, Lermontov tended to
intensify and particularize the emotions and the melodramatic
tone of the works he was imitating. He was not interested in
philosophy or abstract ideas.

Of course, Lermontov did not limit himself to Schiller as a
source for his plays; he commonly took whatever interested him
from a wide variety of sources. His borrowings are particularly
obvious in his first play, *Ispantsy* [The Spaniards, 1830]. The
setting—Spain during the Inquisition—is obviously borrowed
from *Don Carlos,* but the sympathetic treatment of the persecuted
Jews derives from Lessing's famous dramatic poem *Nathan der
Weise* [Nathan the Wise, 1779] and from Sir Walter Scott's
Ivanhoe. Furthermore, it is likely that Lermontov knew of the
great uproar that had broken out in February 1830 when Victor
Hugo's scandalous melodrama *Hernani,* also set in Spain, had
opened in Paris. Spain and also Italy had become very popular
settings for the Romantic poets of northern Europe, and Lermontov was already following this trend by placing the early
versions of his Romantic poem *The Demon* in Spain and by using
both Spain and Italy as settings for other early narrative poems.

The Spaniards is written in blank verse of iambic pentameter
and hexameter. The plot is absurd and the characters unbelievable:
all the Spaniards are heartless villains and all the Jews are kind.
The young man Fernando, an obviously autobiographical figure,
is a foundling who has been brought up in the house of a wealthy
Spaniard, Alvarez. When Alvarez learns that Fernando has had
the temerity to fall in love with his daughter Emilia, he throws
him out. But the chief villain and catalyst of the action is an
Italian Jesuit, Sorrini. Old and outwardly venerable (he is even
in line for a cardinal's hat), he is inwardly a cynical rogue who
maintains a gang of Spaniards to do his bidding.

Angered because Emilia has laughed at him, Sorrini seeks revenge. He bribes her stepmother, Donna Maria, to trick Emilia into attending a supposed rendezvous with Fernando. Then his men bring the unsuspecting Emilia to him. In the best Gothic manner, he prepares to have his way with her as she pleads to the heavens in vain. Enter Fernando. At first disguised as a pilgrim, he soon reveals himself and threatens Sorrini with a dagger, only to admit he cannot stand the sight of blood. Moments later he kills his beloved Emilia in order to save her soul. Sorrini promptly denounces Fernando as a heretic and disciple of Luther, and has him arrested.

As if this were not enough, the play also contains a complicated subplot involving Fernando's Jewish origins. Exhibiting his nobility of character, Fernando saves an old Jew from capture by officers of the Inquisition. Later he is left for dead after being attacked by Sorrini's men, but is discovered and brought home by the same old Jew, Moisey. There he is attended by Moisey's daughter Noemi, who promptly falls in love with him. As in an unwitting parody of a Shakespeare comedy, the denouement reveals that Fernando is really Moisey's son, and therefore Noemi's brother. After a scene in which two gravediggers chat over Emilia's corpse (a clear echo from *Hamlet*), the play ends abruptly when Noemi goes mad over the sudden discovery and impending death of her long-lost brother (an echo of Ophelia's mad scene).

Some of Shakespeare's plots are as far-fetched as this one, but Shakespeare's ear for language saves many of his scenes. Lermontov's characters all speak in the same rhetorical manner, protesting their fate. The speeches of Fernando, Alvarez, his daughter Emilia, his wife, Donna Maria (who later suffers pangs of conscience), Moisey, and his daughter Noemi are virtually interchangeable. The only character of any potential is Sorrini, whose cynical monologues have a snap and bitter humor all too rare in the young Lermontov.

Sorrini in fact dominates the play, for Fernando's actions lack psychological definition and adequate motivation. It is curious that the heroes of Lermontov's plays, unlike those in his narrative poems, do not act decisively in protecting their own interests or in seeking vengeance. Fernando does a great deal of talking, but he does not kill Sorrini or even try to rescue Emilia. After killing his own sweetheart, he makes little effort to escape capture and does not seek vengeance.

There can be no direct influence, of course, but Lermontov's play resembles a mishmash of second-rate Elizabethan revenge tragedies like Thomas Kyd's *The Spanish Tragedy*. Lermontov lacks even Kyd's energy in blood and gore—nothing very much happens in *The Spaniards* except a great deal of declamation. Fernando commits the only murder.

The fact that Lermontov brought this play so near completion but then totally abandoned it, suggests strongly that he realized he could not handle historical melodrama as practiced by Schiller, Hugo, and others. In 1830 and again the following year he made a major shift by setting his next two plays in contemporary Russia. He also wrote them in prose instead of verse. Lermontov drew heavily on his own personal experience in designing both plot and character in them, thus avoiding much of the artificial abstraction of *The Spaniards*. Many serious problems remained unresolved, however.

As though acknowledging Schiller's influence directly, Lermontov gave his second play the German title *Menschen und Leidenschaften: Ein Trauerspiel* [People and Passions: A Tragedy]. The third play is called *Stranny chelovek: Romanticheskaya drama* [The Strange Man: A Romantic Drama, 1831]. The plays have similar plots, and indeed Lermontov transferred some material from the first one to the second.

Both works contain an obvious image of himself. In *People and Passions* he is Yury Volin, and in *The Strange Man,* Vladimir Arbenin. In both plays the hero is again rather ineffectual, easily duped, and quick to despair. Both heroes die at the denouement, just as no doubt Fernando would have if *The Spaniards* had been completed.

People and Passions takes place on the estate of Martha Gromova, a lady of eighty who rules her household with a rod of iron. Her name is based on *grom,* the Russian word for "thunder." Gromova's rough language recalls that of the ignorant landowners in the eighteenth-century satirical comedies of Denis Fonvizin, whose works had just been republished in 1829–30. Gromova's religious fanaticism, anti-Semitism, and mindless chauvinism may originate more with Fonvizin than with Lermontov's grandmother Mme Arsenieva, but there is a clear autobiographical line running through the play. Gromova's grandson Yury Volin (*volya* means "will," and also "freedom") is certainly a self-portrait, although he is five years older than Lermontov was when he wrote the play. The arguments between Gromova and Yury's father over his upbringing may well be based upon those between Mme Arsenieva and Yury Petrovich Lermontov.

The play opens with a time-worn device: a conversation among servants. Besides supplying background information, the servants return from time to time to keep the plot running, and their colloquial language provides a welcome relief from the intensely melodramatic speeches of the main characters. Immediately Zarutsky arrives, a former school friend of Yury's who is now an officer in the Hussars. Quite a lady's man, Zarutsky enlists the help of Yury's cousin and sweetheart Lyubov in approaching her sister Eliza. Yury sees Lyubov and Zarutsky talking quietly together in the garden—so quietly that he cannot hear what they are saying—and jumps to the conclusion that he has been betrayed. He challenges Zarutsky to a duel. Then he abuses Lyubov and tells her he cannot love her anymore. In general Yury behaves like a man possessed, cursing fate and those who have deceived him without giving anyone a chance to explain.

Yury is mistaken in thinking that he has been betrayed by his friend and his sweetheart, but he has indeed been tricked by his uncle, Lyubov's father. The uncle, Vasily Mikhalych, drives a wedge between Yury and his father because he is furious that Yury should pay court to his own cousin. Yury manages to quarrel in succession with his grandmother and his father, who pronounces a curse upon him. This curse shatters Yury even more than Lyubov's supposed perfidy. There is much truth in Yury's complaint that "I have always tried to stop these arguments. . . . Why does everything fall on my head? I am like booty that

is being torn apart by two conquerors; each wants to possess me"
(act 3, scene 2).

Overcome by the loss of both father and sweetheart on the
same day, Yury swallows poison. As the poison takes effect he
talks incoherently to Lyubov:

My friend, there is no hereafter . . . there is chaos . . . it swallows
up tribes . . . we will vanish in chaos, too . . . we will never see
each other again . . . different paths . . . nothingness. . . . Goodbye!
We will never meet again . . . there is no paradise, there is no hell
. . . human beings are cast aside, homeless creatures. (act 5, scene 10)

After this long monologue Yury suffers a crowning blow when
he overhears Eliza and Lyubov talking and learns that his sus-
picions of Lyubov were groundless. Now it is too late, and he
dies.

In *The Strange Man* the hero Vladimir Arbenin suffers a similar
dual betrayal, but he does not commit suicide: he first goes mad,
then dies. In this play the father really is wicked, and the sweetheart, Natasha Zagorskina, really does leave him for his friend
Dmitri Belinsky. In this play once again the central framework
of the plot involves the young hero's destruction by family con-
flicts and an unsuccessful love affair. And, as in the other dramas,
the hero remains essentially passive.

Here the hero's family problems are linked to a conflict between
his father and his mother. His father, Pavel Grigorich, is a cold,
unsympathetic man with little feeling for his son or for his wife,
Maria Dmitrevna. Arbenin vainly pleads with his father to forgive
Maria Dmitrevna, whom the father has divorced for some nameless sin. Pavel Grigorich wavers briefly, but refuses to visit Maria
Dmitrevna even when Arbenin assures him that she is dying of
grief and seeks her husband's forgiveness at the end. Almost on
her deathbed, Maria Dmitrevna confesses to Arbenin that she had
had an affair. When she told Pavel Grigorich about this lapse
and sought his understanding, he drove her from the house.

Arbenin suffers equal failure in his relationship with Natasha:
though he swears undying devotion to her, she prefers his best
friend, Belinsky, who reciprocates her feelings and proposes mar-

riage. Belinsky justifies this action by arguing to himself (though not to Arbenin) that he is doing Arbenin a favor. Arbenin's situation is not helped by the fact that Natasha's cousin, Princess Sophia, is in love with him and so consistently presents him in a bad light to Natasha. Later on, Sophia repents of her deception. She criticizes society, feels doomed, and questions her own motives: "Can it be that I have two hearts, so that one and the same thing cause me both joy and anguish?" (scene 12). Earlier, as her doubts intensified, Sophia had tried to reassure herself: "People are not guilty if fate inadvertently fulfills their evil desires. That means they are just, that means my heart should be calm, should have been calm!" (scene 9). This is the germ of an idea developed by Pechorin in *A Hero of Our Time*: one justifies the exercise of one's will by pointing to the inevitability of fate.

When Arbenin hears rumors of Natasha's engagement he rushes to see her, but it is too late. As a typical Lermontovian hero, Arbenin flies into a rage and vows vengeance. Like Yury Volin, Arbenin interprets this betrayal by his sweetheart as evidence of the direct interference of God in his affairs:

God! God! I no longer have faith in you or feel any love for you! . . . Why did you give me a fiery heart that loves to excess but cannot hate to the same degree! You are guilty! Let your thunder descend upon my disobedient head: I doubt whether the final howl of a dying worm would give you much pleasure! (scene 12)

But God has still other blows in reserve. Arbenin's mother dies, and the funeral is held on the same day Natasha's engagement is announced. Arbenin tells Natasha he will not play the part of Werther to her Charlotte, curses Belinsky, and rushes out. We do not see him again.

The thirteenth and final scene, the "Epilogue," is set three months later. Guests at a soiree given by a Count N discuss the latest society gossip, including the wedding of Natasha and Belinsky, which is to take place the following day. Natasha is referred to as a coquette, and Arbenin's father is praised as "an honorable man in all respects." A series of nameless but numbered guests discuss Arbenin's madness and personality. The Third

Guest repeatedly defends Arbenin, commenting on the promising manuscripts found in his room and expressing sympathy for him: "His heart matured before his mind; he learned the evil side of life before he was able to guard against its attacks, or endure them with equanimity."

A note arrives from Pavel Grigorich announcing the death of his son, who will be buried on the next day, the same day as the wedding of his former sweetheart and former friend. Clearly in the Gothic tradition, this juxtaposition of marriage and death strikes one as a little contrived.

The Strange Man is an improvement on *People and Passions* in several ways, however. In general, Lermontov paints a larger canvas and permits a more varied range of people to participate in the dialogue, if not in the action. There are some strong scenes in which the servants talk in a lively, colloquial style, providing a different perspective on the main characters. When Arbenin flees the scene after his mother's death, the servant calmly reflects that now everything that once belonged to her mistress is hers.

Lermontov also understands that he need not present every traumatic moment on stage. The final climactic argument between father and son—when Pavel Grigorich curses Arbenin much as the father curses Volin in *People and Passions*—is reported; and Arbenin's death takes place off stage.

The high-society scenes exhibit Lermontov's talent for satire and quick characterization (or perhaps caricature) brought to maturity in his ironical narrative poems and his prose fiction. Scene 4, in which Arbenin's fellow Moscow University students drink and talk in his absence about a disappointing performance of Schiller's *The Robbers,* has some possibilities, but soon they are reciting and admiring some of Arbenin's verses, an imitation of Byron's "The Dream."

This latter scene points up a serious weakness remaining from Lermontov's first two plays: the author is too ready to concoct scenes and speeches which present his pet ideas, instead of allowing the dialogue and the action to be determined by the psychology of the characters. Paradoxically, he maintains a close grip on his material, and yet lacks proper esthetic control over it. The result is confusion in the reader's mind.

Soviet critics have traditionally viewed *The Strange Man* as an attack on serfdom. Such a view distorts the evidence. To begin with, the "attack" occurs in only part of scene 5. Second, it is undercut by the author, who evidently considers his hero's plight more desperate than that of the serfs. After expressing outrage at the treatment of serfs by a brutal woman landowner, Arbenin declares:

There are people more worthy of pity than that peasant. External misfortunes will pass, but a man who bears deep in his heart the cause of all his sufferings has his every last spark of pleasure devoured by worms. A man who desires and hopes . . . he is a burden even to those who love him.

To Belinsky's reasonable question: "How can one compare a free man with a slave?" Arbenin replies firmly:

One is the slave of man, the other is the slave of fate. The first can hope for a good master or has some choice, but the other has none; he is the plaything of blind chance, and his passions and the insensibility of others jointly lead to his destruction.

Certain features in Lermontov's three early plays recall the novels of one of the greatest of Russian writers: Fyodor Dostoevsky. Lermontov's emotional tone, the frantic rages, the accusations and sudden changes of mood, the juxtaposition of marriage with death—all find echoes in Dostoevsky's works. Dostoevsky drew upon the Gothic novel, Schiller's early *Sturm und Drang* melodramas, the works of the *école frénétique,* and later Utopian Socialists in France as his sources. But Dostoevsky can make these elements work—while in Lermontov's plays, and in the Gothic novels, they remain strident and unconvincing—because he has complete control of his material by the use of his narrator.[6]

Lermontov's narrative poems and plays of the Moscow period portray the author himself in various situations, imagined and real. The heroes' monologues are in most cases very similar to

the lyrics and short poems that Lermontov was writing at about
the same time. This is particularly true in *The Strange Man,* where
Lermontov dramatized his unhappy relationship with Natalya
Ivanova, clearly the central figure of his emotional life in 1831
and early 1832.

The Lyrics

Lermontov wrote nearly 300 short poems from 1828 to 1832,
but their range of tone and subject matter is very narrow. The
majority of them are love lyrics, addressed to the beloved; there
are only a few examples of nature poetry or *poésie descriptive.*

The lack of nature poems during this period is perhaps not
surprising: Lermontov was living in Moscow most of the time,
and the countryside around Serednikovo seems to have attracted
his attention far less than the charms of Ekaterina Sushkova and
Natalya Ivanova. Furthermore, Lermontov was not a northern
poet: only the luxuriant flora and fauna of the South inspired
him. Lermontov never attempted the beautiful descriptions of
winter scenes and the wooded area of central Russia left us by
Pushkin.

On those rare occasions when Lermontov describes nature, he
does so in generalized terms in order to draw the inevitable
parallel with the situation of the lyrical hero: thus in "Solntse
oseni" [The Autumn Sun] he likens the decline in the warmth
of the sun to the heart of one who has been misunderstood and
therefore cannot love again.

At this point, Lermontov deals mostly in stereotypes when
describing nature or the seasons, usually introduced in similes.
A frequent example is the simile of the windblown leaf, as in the
poem beginning "Give me your hand, lean on the poet's breast."
The poet closes with a typical complaint about his isolation,
which he explains as follows:

> Thus the bush grows above the sea's abyss
> And the leaf, torn off by the storm, floats
> According to the whim of the wandering waters. (1:286)

Lermontov did write a few "think pieces" which touch upon current social and political topics, but even here he usually focuses less on the objective situation than on the lyrical hero and his feelings. The ostensible subject only has validity in so far as it is related to the poet.

As a schoolboy still feeling his way, Lermontov at first used generic titles for his short poems: ballad, madrigal, romance, elegy, song. He soon became more independent, however, and paid little attention to genre distinctions, especially in the short form. As the chief Romantic poet in Russian literature, Lermontov intensified and accelerated the move toward the use of poetry as a means of self-examination and self-expressionn.

Like any normal person, Lermontov was interested in the political events of his time, but he makes only scattered references to them in his poetry. Like Pushkin, he supported the struggle for political freedom, except when the struggle was against Russia. For example, Lermontov advised the Causasian tribes to submit to Russian arms, and did not sympathize with the Polish insurrection of November 1830. In his comment on the Paris uprising of July 1830, Lermontov primarily berated Charles X for not taking advantage of his chances to be a good king ("30 iyunya" [June 30]).

Living under the oppressive regime of Nicholas I, Lermontov was understandably slow to exhibit suspect tendencies. But he was much less of a civic poet than even Pushkin, not to mention the Decembrist Kondraty Ryleev, who dedicated his talents to the cause of political reform. Care must be taken not to read into Lermontov's early poetry political sentiments which they do not contain. Some Soviet commentators succumb too readily to this temptation.

I will cite just one cautionary example: Lermontov's poem of 1831 "Iz Andreya Shenie" [From André Chénier] (1:287). The notes to this poem in the latest Soviet edition of Lermontov's work (1979) claim that it is one of a series of poems written at this time in response to "peasant uprisings in Russia, the national liberation movement of peoples in the Caucasus, and revolutionary events in Europe" (1:578). It is quite true that André Chénier had become, in Russia as elsewhere, a symbol of the poet's fight

for freedom. But it is also true that Chénier was a liberal mon-
archist, not a revolutionary. He did not fall victim to the *ancien
régime* in France; on the contrary, he was guillotined in 1794
during the Terror by those whom he accused of betraying the
revolution. What attracted the Romantics to Chénier was not his
call to revolution but his concept of the poet as the conscience
of mankind; he reminds us of Shelley's statement in *A Defence of
Poetry* that "Poets are the unacknowledged legislators of the
world."

No source in Chénier's poetry has been found for Lermontov's
poem, but it would be characteristic of Lermontov to "fuse" ideas,
or use Chénier's work as a springboard for his own feelings. The
poem consists of just twenty lines. It begins with the couplet:

> Perhaps I will fall on behalf of the general cause
> Or I will spend my life fruitlessly in exile.

What the "general cause" *(obshchee delo)* might be is unclear,
but the rest of the poem is devoted to a familiar litany of problems
and declarations of devotion to a nameless "friend."

> Perhaps, struck down by cunning slander,
> Humiliated by foes before the world and you,
> I will not take off the crown woven with shame
> And will myself seek an untimely death;
> But do not blame the young sufferer,
> I pray, do not speak mocking words.
> My terrible destiny is worthy of your tears,
> I have done much evil, but have endured more.
> Maybe I am guilty before my proud enemies,
> Let them seek revenge; in my heart, I swear by
>   the heavens,
> I am not a villain; oh no, fate has destroyed me;
> I bared my breast, I sacrificed myself;
> Bored by the vanity of the deceptive world,
> I could not help but keep my solemn vow;
> I may have brought much harm to society,
> But I have always been true to you, my friend, always;

> Alone, or 'midst the rebellious crowd,
> I always loved you and loved you so tenderly. (1:287)

The maudlin self-pity, the references to justifiable sins, the call for sympathy and love, the paranoia, and the deliberate mystification—all are typical of Lermontov's juvenilia, as is the low quality of the verse. The poem has nothing to do with national liberation movements, peasant uprisings in Russia, or the overthrow of Charles X.

One of the longest poems Lermontov wrote during this period is entitled "1831-go iyunya 11 dnya" [June 11, 1831] (1:167–75) and consists of thirty-two stanzas of eight lines each. Complaining that "cold letters" cannot convey the fervor he feels, Lermontov runs through a series of reminiscences, regrets, passionate yearnings, and the like—a sort of compilation of the motifs recurring throughout his poetry of this period, and even later.

In stanza 22 he insists he needs to act, because "life is so boring when there is no struggle." In the next stanza he senses that he has little time. and in stanza 28 he foretells his own early death. He returned to this uneasy feeling several times in his brief life:

> And I shall not die forgotten. My death
> Will be terrible; foreign lands
> Will wonder at it, but in my native land
> All will curse even a recollection of me.

In stanza 24 Lermontov offers an interesting and uncharacteristic confession:

> You find the root of your torments in yourself,
> It makes no sense to blame heaven for anything.

In the next stanza, he displays in embryo the psychological insight so striking in his novel *A Hero of Our Time*:

> I became accustomed to this situation,
> But it could not be expressed clearly
> By either angelic or demonic language:
> They do not know such anxieties.

> In one all is pure, and in the other all is evil.
> Only in man does one find
> The holy linked to the depraved. All his
> Torments result from this.

For now, however, Lermontov was not ready to make use of this perception.

Love lyrics, usually addressed to the beloved by the male poet, form the majority of Lermontov's short poems at this period. Very frequently the poet asks the beloved to share his view of this world as a vale of tears, and he always complains of his own accursed fate. Often enough he reproaches her for "betraying" his innocent, selfless love. The opening lines of a poem of 1831 addressed to Ivanova are typical in their banality:

> I am not worthy, perhaps,
> Of your love: it is not for me to judge;
> But you have rewarded with deceit
> My hopes and dreams,
> And I will always say that you
> Have acted unjustly. (1:194)

In 1829 Lermontov wrote his first poem on the idea of the demon, which was to play a central role in his brief literary career. The short work of sixteen lines is called "Moy demon" [My Demon] (1:52). Flying among the clouds, the demon is described as liking storms, rivers, and the rustle of oak groves. But he is also gloomy, and spends his time sowing evil and distrust.

Some time afterwards—probably in late 1831—Lermontov reworked this poem, retaining only its first four lines. The revised version consists of four stanzas of eight lines each. The final stanza is the most interesting, as the poet enters the scene to declare his own feelings about the demon:

> And the proud demon will be with me
> As long as I live
> And it will come to illumine my mind
> With rays of heavenly fire;
> It will show me the image of perfection

> And suddenly take it away forever,
> And, after giving me a foretaste of bliss,
> It will never give me happiness again. (1:293)

The young man who wrote these lines was certainly not play-acting. They lack the sure artistic touch that he developed a few years later, but even here we feel the dynamism of his vision. Lermontov was right about the strength of the hold the image of the Demon had upon him, but he did finally free himself from it.

In 1832 Lermontov wrote a short poem very probably addressed to Varvara Lopukhina, whose image he long associated with the innocent girl who attracts the Demon's notice:

> Listen, perhaps when we have abandoned
> Forever this world, which so chills our souls,
> Perhaps, in a land where deceit is unknown,
> You will be an angel and I will become a devil! (1:327)

Many of the poems Lermontov wrote to Varenka were lost in the same way as those to Natalya Ivanova: they were destroyed by a jealous husband. The few to have survived demonstrate Lermontov's ability to write love poems celebrating the spiritual and emotional qualities of a woman his own age in addition to her physical charms. Probably the best poem he wrote to her at this time is only sixteen lines long (1:341). It begins:

> Not by her proud beauty does she
> Entice lively youths.
>   . . . .
> But her voice penetrates the soul
> Like the remembrance of better days,
> And the heart loves and suffers,
> Almost ashamed of its love.

Once again one senses here Lermontov's true feelings at that time in his life.

The overall impression Lermontov's early poems make, however, as the critic Eugène Duchesne noted at the beginning of this century, is one of a "monotonie fatigante."[7] It must be added, in fairness, that Lermontov soon became his own severest critic. When in 1840 he was preparing a collection of his poetry for publication, he excluded everything he had written during his Moscow period.

Lermontov did, however, make one exception, for his now famous poem "Angel" [The Angel]. (1:213). Readers ever since have agreed that it is a fine poem, and it represents very well one important aspect of Lermontov's personality and poetry.

The poem describes an angel singing a gentle song in praise of Paradise as he flies at midnight across the heavens, bearing in his embrace a young soul to the world of "sadness and tears." The soul remains on earth for a long time, remembering the heavenly song, which "the boring songs of the earth" cannot replace. The story is told in the past tense, which reinforces the narrative form, and entirely in the third person, but clearly the lyrical tone is paramount.

The poem consists of four quatrains written in a ternary meter: the amphibrachs that Lermontov used more widely and with greater finesse than any other major poet of that period or later. He alternates three-foot and four-foot lines, dropping the final unstressed syllable, so that the rhyme is masculine throughout. Every stanza consists of two rhyming couplets, each forming a separate phrase: that is, enjambement occurs only after the first and third lines, not after the second. Lermontov begins five of the poem's sixteen lines with "And," but their lilting rhythm carries the reader along so that he scarcely notices this potential weakness.

In his famous essay *Über naïve und sentimentalische Dichtung* [On Naive and Sentimental Poetry, 1795] Friedrich Schiller wrote that "sentimental," or modern, poetry could be divided into three kinds: satire, in which the poet looks down upon reality from the position of the Ideal; elegy, in which the poet mourns the loss of the Ideal; and idyll, in which the poet imagines the Ideal as a reality, either as past Golden Age or future Utopia. Much of Lermontov's early poetry fits the second and third categories, with emphasis on the second.

Another aspect of Lermontov's poetry took on increasing importance, however, during the latter years of the Moscow period and began even to dominate later: aggressive demonism and rebelliousness, the idealist's response to the frustration of his dreams. Hence the theme of vengeance in his narrative poems and plays.

In 1832 Lermontov began to exhibit signs of independence, both from his relationship with Natalya Ivanova and from Byron's domination of his poetic personality. His poem to Ivanova beginning "I will not humble myself before you" demonstrates his growing dissatisfaction with the role of supplicant (1:308). Another poem of 1832, "No, I Am Not Byron, I Am Different," attempts to define his own poetic individuality, although Lermontov makes this declaration in terms that remind us very much of Byron (1:321):

> Like him I am a wanderer hounded by the world,
> But I have a Russian soul.

Later in this short poem the poet employs a typical comparison with the turbulent ocean:

> Oh gloomy ocean, who can
> Plumb your secrets? Who
> Will relate to the crowd my thoughts?
> I—or God—or no one!

The only other poem among Lermontov's early juvenilia to have gained the esteem of later generations, even though Lermontov himself did not publish it in his lifetime, is "Parus" [The Sail] (1:347)[8] which utilizes the Romantic symbol of the restless sea. This short lyric illustrates the other, more dynamic and rebellious side of Lermontov's poetic personality.

Though written shortly after Lermontov arrived in St. Petersburg in the late summer of 1832, the poem belongs in spirit to his Moscow period. Lermontov enclosed the poem in a letter he wrote in September to his favorite correspondent, Maria Lopukhina.

Like "The Angel," "The Sail" omits the first-person pronoun completely. But instead of telling a story, it presents a series of scenes in which the sail symbolizes rebellious youth. The poem consists of three quatrains in iambic tetrameters with aBaB rhyme scheme.[9] In each stanza the first two lines offer a straightforward description of the scene, while the second two provide the commentary and personify the sail as a man (the word for "sail" is masculine in Russian). Lines 3 and 4 of the first stanza pose two questions:

> What does it seek in a distant country?
> What has it abandoned in its native land?

A negative reply is given in lines 3 and 4 of the second stanza:

> Alas! It does not seek happiness
> And it is not fleeing from happiness.

The poem's concluding lines, though they make a definite statement about the sail, do not respond to the questions:

> But, rebellious, it seeks the storm,
> As though calm could be found in storms!

The first two lines of each stanza seem to describe a scene at a different time of year, or at least under different weather conditions. In the first we find mist; in the second a fierce wind blows; in the third the sun shines brightly on a bright blue sea. But this pleasant weather leaves the sail dissatisfied: it yearns for the storm as a way out of its puzzling dilemma.

In much the same way, Lermontov remained dissatisfied with both his personal and poetic life. His solution was to abandon his literary pursuits temporarily and to seek the storm, in the form of a military career.

Chapter Three
"Rebel Without a Cause": St. Petersburg (1832–37)

Literature of the Caucasus

Some of Lermontov's acquaintances recalled that, while in St. Petersburg as student and cadet, Lermontov loved to sketch views of the Caucasus and the Circassians native to that region. Lermontov did not limit himself to sketching, however: he also described his subjects in verse. While at cavalry school he wrote two narrative poems, both set in the Caucasus. *Aul Bastundzhi* (a place name) and *Khadzhi Abrek* (a man's name) recall the works of Lermontov's Moscow period. In them we find the same lavish descriptions of the scenery, the same violent passions, and the same strong, but scarcely silent, heroes.

One thing has changed: Lermontov has become perceptibly more skillful in handling his material. The verse is more mature, less strained. *Aul Bastundzhi* is, in fact, written in *ottava rima* (stanzas of eight lines with the rhyme scheme AbAbAbCC). Lermontov was one of the first and most skillful Russian poets to write a long poem in this stanzaic form. The poem consists of four stanzas of dedication to the Caucasus itself, and then two parts, the first of forty-two stanzas and the second of thirty-four (2:212–32). The plot involves a love triangle, with two brothers as rivals in passion, when Selim falls in love with Zara, the wife of his older brother Akbulat. In a long speech Selim confesses his passion to Akbulat and declares it would be best for his brother to kill him, because he will never cease to love Zara. Akbulat declines while warning his brother sternly that he will not yield what belongs to him. Selim leaves.

In Part II Selim returns to accost Zara as she is bathing in a mountain stream. In a lengthy speech he declares his undying love and begs her to come away with him. Zara rejects his plea, for she is true to Akbulat. Time passes. Next we see Akbulat returning to his home at Aul Bastundzhi to discover that both his wife and his favorite horse are missing. Soon afterwards the horse arrives bearing Zara's dead body. Akbulat curses Selim, and the narrator closes with a coda picturing Aul Bastundzhi, now long forgotten.

The rivalry between the brothers recalls a Schillerian motif which Lermontov would explore again in his prose play *Dva brata* [Two Brothers, 1836]. Later on Lermontov returns to a variation of this motif in the rivalry between Pechorin and Grushnitsky in *A Hero of Our Time,* and here he handles it with great psychological insight. In this poem the verbal exchanges between characters can hardly be called dialogue. In the first part Selim delivers long monologues to which Akbulat responds with briefer statements; in the second part, Selim delivers more long monologues to which Zara responds with briefer statements. Only once—in the sixteenth stanza of Part II—does Lermontov introduce a series of quick remarks that constitute genuine dialogue.

Much the same may be said of *Khadzhi Abrek,* except that here the narrative is occasionally interrupted by speeches in the form of dialogue, as in a play (2:233–45). This is reminiscent of Byron's so-called "closet dramas," which Pushkin had earlier imitated. Indeed, *Khadzhi Abrek* owes a great deal to Byron's *The Giaour.* It is written in iambic tetrameters, with various rhyming schemes: there are mostly couplets, but also some alternating and enclosed rhymes.

Lermontov must have been pleased with this poem, because he showed it to his professor of literature at the cavalry school. The professor reportedly was so impressed that he told the class it exhibited great promise. Lermontov was, however, extremely chagrined when *Khadzhi Abrek* suddenly appeared in print in August 1835: one of his many relatives had filched a copy and passed it along to the editor of the popular journal *Biblioteka dlya chteniya* [Library for Reading]. Shan-Girey reports that Lermontov calmed down only after nobody attacked the poem. *Khadzhi Abrek* thus became Lermontov's first work to be published, if we overlook a very short poem that he published in 1830 over the Latin letter "L."

The setting of *Khadzhi Abrek* is again the Caucasus. An old man bewails the loss of his three sons in battle and two daughters taken by brigands; now only one daughter remains alive. He asks for a volunteer to recover this daughter back from her kidnapper, Bey-Bulat. Khadzhi volunteers. He locates the daughter, Leila, who tells him she is quite happy living with Bey-Bulat and has no intention of returning to her father's village. Then Khadzhi tells Leila the real reason for his having volunteered to help the old man. Bey-Bulat had once ambushed Khadzhi's brother, killing him like an animal. Khadzhi vowed revenge, but then considered that killing Bey-Bulat would be too painless: he wanted Bey-Bulat to suffer. So he decided to wait until Bey-Bulat had fallen in love, and then kill his beloved. Leila pleads for her life in vain. The cold-hearted Khadzhi cuts off her head and delivers it to her grief-stricken father. A year later the bodies of two richly dressed men are found; they have killed each other:

> One was recognized as Bey-Bulat,
> No one knew the other.

In this poem Lermontov shows considerable skill in his handling of meter and rhyme, but his ability is wasted on inadequate material. For a long time Lermontov could not seem to extricate himself from these tales of blood and thunder set against the exotic scenery of the Caucasus. Hereafter, though, he never returned to the "Eastern tale." His two most famous Caucasian poems, *Mtsyri* [The Novice] and *Demon* [The Demon], written or completed toward the end of his life, are very different from these tales of vengeance and intrigue.

The Reversion to Russia

In his remaining works of this period, Lermontov evidently decided to employ Russian settings, both historical and contemporary. Until this point he had rarely used even Russian historical material in his narrative poems. (An exception is "Posledny syn volnosti" [The Last Son of Freedom], a poem about events in medieval Novgorod, dating from late 1830 or early 1831.) His two autobiographical plays, on the other hand—*People and Passions* and *The Strange Man*—are set in contemporary Russia. Lermontov now set his next narrative poem—*Boyarin Orsha* [The Boyar Orsha]—and his first attempt at prose fiction—*Vadim*—in the Russian past. But then the historical setting is not of great significance in either work. In fact, Lermontov simply transferred to Russian characters and Russian backgrounds the style and themes he had already explored in non-Russian settings.

Both works are typically Lermontovian conglomerations, heavily influenced by his own earlier narrative poems, by Gothic novels, and by Byron. *The Boyar Orsha,* written in 1835–36, includes passages cannibalized from a narrative poem of 1830, *Ispoved* [A Confession]; in its turn, it would serve in 1839 as the basis for Lermontov's much more famous narrative poem *Mtsyri* [The Novice]. The plot of *The Boyar Orsha* takes place during the reign of Ivan the Terrible in the sixteenth century, but the quasi-historical setting is far less important for the poem than are Byron's works from which Lermontov draws the epigraphs for the three "chapters" (2:246–74).

Orsha, a longtime favorite of the Tsar, is finally released from court service and allowed to return to his home on the Dnieper River, which then marked the southern boundary of Muscovy. One stormy night the suspicious Orsha hears whispering in the bedroom of his beautiful daughter, who is never named. Her lover, Arseny, is telling her of his plans to take her away with him and his band of warrior friends. Orsha has Arseny arrested, then locks his daughter in a tower and hurls the key into the river. Chapter 2 is set in a nearby monastery, where Arseny is being held in chains. Orsha and the Father Superior visit him to find him unrepentant, even defiant. It turns out that Arseny had been brought as a foundling to the monastery and had entered Orsha's service. Orsha threatens Arseny with punishment for his ingratitude:

> I will repay you, villain,
> You foundling without a cross,
> Despicable slave and orphan! (2:259)

Arseny replies that he has been held against his wishes, that he was "In soul a child, by fate a monk." When asked to reveal the names of his band of friends, who appear to be brigands, Arseny refuses even under the threat of torture. At the end of this section Arseny is rescued from the monastery by his friends and flees with them across the Dnieper to the territory of Russia's enemies, the Lithuanians and Poles.

Chapter 3 opens with a description of wolves prowling near the frozen Dnieper. Orsha has raised troops to repel a Lithuanian attack. As the troops move against the enemy, Orsha alone does not cross himself and pray. The narrator comments that he is "like a Moslem, like a Tatar prince" in a broad hint to the reader that Orsha recognizes his guilt in locking up his daughter to die.

During the battle, Arseny, who has joined the Lithuanians, encounters the mortally wounded Orsha. Orsha curses him as a traitor and regrets that he cannot avenge himself, but does tell Arseny where his daugher is, and even urges him to rescue her quickly, for she is waiting for Arseny now. Orsha dies and Arseny rushes back to the locked castle, where he finds his beloved's skeleton. He first complains of his fate like a typical Byronic hero:

> Yes, I am a criminal, I am a villain,
> But is my punishment equal to my crime?

Then he calls upon God to return to him his beloved's tender glance:

> Without her what is the earth and paradise?
> They are merely hollow sounding words:
> A magnificent temple without a divinity. (2:273–74)

The Boyar Orsha is written in iambic tetrameter, by far the most popular meter of nineteenth-century verse, and Lermontov demonstrates once again his growing facility in the handling of meter and rhyme. He divided the poem into "chapters" rather than into stanzas in order to place greater emphasis on plot and narrative structure. But still, at this stage in his development too much poetic skill chases too little plot. He still draws upon the works of others for character types and skeletal plots. These problems still haunt him, even when he turns to prose for the first time in *Vadim* (4:7–109).

Vadim

Lermontov worked on *Vadim* from 1832 until 1834. He did not complete it, and we do not know if he intended to include it in a projected trilogy of historical novels set at various periods in Russian history which he mentioned to friends in the last years of his life. *Vadim* was evidently one of the secret projects Lermontov worked on while still a cadet at the cavalry school. Alexander Merinsky says Lermontov told him he had completed three chapters of a novel set in the reign of Catherine II, and based in part "on a real incident, according to accounts by his grandmother" (*Vosp.,* 133). If there was in fact such an incident, it does not lend Lermontov's draft any putative realism.

The plot involves Vadim's search for vengeance against a neighboring landowner, Boris Palitsyn. Some time earlier, Palitsyn had seized property belonging to Vadim's father and caused his premature death. Vadim's sister Olga has been brought up as Palitsyn's ward. Vadim falls in love with his own sister, but she herself loves Palitsyn's son Yury. Thus, in the familiar triangle, two men struggle for the affections of the heroine, who remains a rather pale figure. Once rejected by Olga, Vadim seeks dual vengeance, against both father and son.

Vadim is an extreme outsider. He escapes the cloister to become a beggar. He is a hunchback with bowed legs. Vadim decides to join the peasant rebellion as a means of gaining revenge upon the Palitsyns and taking their land, which includes his own father's property. Lermontov did not complete the story, so we do not know whether Vadim would have succeeded. But by the end of the manuscript he is already more monster than hero, recalling the demonic figures of the Gothic novels and some of Byron's poems. In other words, during the course of the story Vadim moves from wronged innocent to aggressive destroyer in a development that parallels on a much more vicious level the changes in Lermontov's own personality. Vadim is, in fact, a projection of some aspects of Lermontov's character, and the novel is a vehicle for some of his pet ideas.

Vadim illustrates very well both Lermontov's lack of interest in history and the dangers of exaggerating genre distinctions in his juvenilia. Although written in prose, *Vadim* resembles Lermontov's youthful narrative poems in the character of its hero-villain, its central theme of vengeance, its feminine characters (innocent, naive virgins), its violence, and the melodramatic stridency of its language. In fact, there are many direct borrowings from earlier poems in *Vadim,* especially in the hero's monologues. At the same time, the narrative approach varies considerably, as melodramatic monologues give way to chatty asides to the reader. The failure to establish a single narrative point of view is a serious weakness in *Vadim.*

It makes little sense to call *Vadim* a historical novel. Although set during the Pugachyov Rebellion, the rebellion itself has no social or political significance, but is merely a vehicle for Vadim's private purposes. Lermontov includes no historical personages, and his fictional characters are not believable.

Perhaps Lermontov realized this: in any case he abandoned both *Vadim* and prose fiction for a couple of years. He returned instead to verse narratives, where he felt more at home, and also resumed his attempts at playwriting.

The Masquerade

Lermontov's verse drama *Maskarad* [The Masquerade] was the first fruit of the "move into society" of which he once wrote to Maria Lopukhina.[1] The initial idea for the play came to him during the winter of 1834–35. Among the balls he attended then were some given by the enormously wealthy Vasily Engelhardt, who is mentioned by name in the play.

Lermontov wrote his play in what are known as "free iambs" (*volny iamb*), taking his example from Alexander Griboedov's famous play *Gore ot umá* [Woe from Wit], which had appeared in a censored version in 1833. That is, the meter of *Masquerade* is iambic, but the lines may vary in length from one syllable to a dozen, and rhyming varies also. Lermontov followed Griboedov's example in writing a play that includes much satire directed against St. Petersburg high society.

The play's central character is Evgeny Arbenin: Lermontov gives this name again to a Byronic figure who is in part a projection of himself as a man in his late thirties. Arbenin has recently married a lovely young girl, Nastasia Pavlovna (called Nina), after abandoning his earlier wayward life of gambling and carousing. In 1.3.1 Arbenin says he has married out of boredom, so that he would no longer have to engage in tiresome love affairs where, as he says, "before beginning the novel, I already knew the denouement." Much to his surprise, Arbenin falls in love with his wife, who represents his salvation from old torments and doubts. In effect Nina represents Arbenin's "good self," in a recasting of Lermontov's relationship with Varvara Lopukhina.

Though he claims to have "arisen [*voskres*] for life and goodness" (1.3.3) Arbenin has no faith in Nina at a moment of crisis which ensues. In the opening scene Arbenin saves Prince Zvezdich from ruin in a card game. At a ball at Engelhardt's, a mysterious masked lady flirts with the Prince and gives him a bracelet which Nina had dropped accidentally. The Prince tells Arbenin the whole story, and of course shows him the bracelet.

As Arbenin awaits Nina's return from the masquerade he is in a bad mood: "It used to be that other men's wives waited for me," he says. "Now I am waiting for my own wife" (1.3.2). When Arbenin sees that she has lost one of her pair of matching bracelets, he immediately concludes that Nina has been unfaithful. He becomes enraged and generally behaves like Othello with Desdemona: "Listen, Nina . . . I was born/With a soul that seethes like lava" (1.3.5), he cries. Nina's protests are in vain.

We learn later that the woman who flirted with Prince Zvezdich was the Baroness Strahl. The Baroness reads the novels of George Sand, already famous for her advanced views on the rights of women to sexual and economic independence. Lermontov's baroness has presumably adopted a similarly exciting life-style in the stuffy salons of St. Petersburg. Baroness Strahl discovers what has happened, but decides to keep quiet so as not to damage her own reputation.

Prince Zvezdich believes that Nina is the woman he is seeking and immediately lays siege to her honor. Arbenin intercepts a note from him which confirms Arbenin's worst fears, and he now plots revenge against the two of them. Even a sudden and unmotivated attempt by Baroness Strahl to tell the truth does not deflect him from his purpose.

Instead of challenging the Prince to a duel, Arbenin invites him to cards at the apartment of a mutual friend. He takes total revenge in a simple but effective way, by bringing into play the unwritten code of high society. When the Prince wins a hand at cards, Arbenin loudly accuses him of cheating and hurls his cards in the Prince's face. Arbenin refuses to fight a duel, so that the Prince cannot clear his honor. Zvezdich admits defeat and decides to leave for the Caucasus.

Arbenin's revenge against his wife is much more drastic: he poisons her ice cream at a ball. He first justifies himself before God:

> Forgive her, bless her—
> But I am not God and I do not forgive! (3.1.2)

Yet he considers taking poison and dying with her:

> [She has drunk] All of it! All of it!
> Not a drop left for me! How cruel! (3.1.4)

The conversation between Arbenin and Nina, as she dies slowly of the poison, is ghoulish. When she complains of illness and asks for a doctor, Arbenin launches into a peroration on the vanity of human existence. Later, when Nina realizes what has happened

and says she is dying, Arbenin replies: "So soon? No, not yet.
There's half an hour to go" (3.2.2). When Nina protests she does
not want to die, Arbenin laughs: "I just knew that would bother
you."

A moment later Arbenin is crying and claiming he loves her.
But Nina curses him before she dies, as she continues to maintain
her innocence.

At this point Lermontov's original version of the play ended:
Arbenin is troubled but triumphant after taking double revenge
against his supposedly deceitful wife and his quite definitely
ungrateful friend. This manuscript has not survived, but the
records of the theater censorship show that in October 1835
Lermontov submitted a play in three acts, asking that it be passed
for performance at the Imperial Theater of St. Petersburg. The
play was rejected, and on 8 November Lermontov's manuscript
was returned to him for "necessary changes."

Lermontov must have been disappointed by the rejection, and
certainly he did not care for the type of changes suggested. The
censor, August Oldekop, objected to Arbenin's throwing cards
in the face of Prince Zvezdich, and thought it in very poor taste
to satirize the balls at Engelhardt's. Lermontov reacted by going
over the censor's head. He visited a friend, Andrey Muravyov,
whose cousin Alexander Mordvinov was a high official in the so-
called Third Section, and asked him to intercede on his behalf.
Mordvinov refused to cooperate.

The office of the theater censorship, like its other branches,
was attached to the Third Section of His Imperial Majesty's Personal Chancery. The Third Section was established by Tsar Nicholas I in 1826, immediately after he assumed the throne, and
during his reign remained the single most powerful branch of
government, with its secret spies and informers, as well as officials
in uniform known as gendarmes. In setting up this fearsome
office, Nicholas was following the recommendation of General
Count Alexander Benckendorff, who served as Chief of the Corps
of Gendarmes from its inception until his death in 1844.

The prevalence of German-sounding names in the civil service
stemmed from Russian aristocrats' disdain for government service

at that time. This attitude, together with the extremely Prussian temperament of Nicholas I, led to the appointment of many men of German origin, particularly of Baltic-German origin, to positions of great power in his government.

Thus in Lermontov's case a German censor named Oldekop used French to take a Russian writer to task for denigrating Russian morals!

Count Benckendorff himself felt obliged to express opinions on manuscripts submitted for approval, and his comments on Lermontov's play reveal the general approach of the censorship at that time. It was concerned first with maintaining proper moral tone and social decorum, and to a lesser degree with blocking what it considered subversive political ideas. What it thought subversive, however, would have been considered anywhere else mere discussion of socio-philosophical questions.

Benckendorff questioned the ending of Lermontov's play, which, he thought, "glorifies vice" by allowing Arbenin to go free after the murder of his wife. Benckendorff, a notorious womanizer, suggested that the ending be changed so that "Mr. and Mrs. Arbenin can be reconciled."

Lermontov drew the line at Benckendorff's suggestion, but did respond to the general thrust of the censorship's objections. He added a fourth act in which, the day after the murder, Arbenin is penitent:

> . . . I desired happiness
> And God sent me happiness in the form of an angel. (4.1.5)

Arbenin is then exposed as a murderer and informed of his tragic mistake in suspecting Nina of infidelity. In the end he goes mad.

Lermontov managed to alter his ending ingeniously, if artificially, by introducing a new character known simply as The Stranger to resolve the situation satisfactorily. It turns out that The Stranger had been ruthlessly fleeced of all his possessions while playing cards with Arbenin seven years previously. He decided to devote all his energies to watching Arbenin and awaiting an opportunity for revenge. He had observed Arbenin putting poison in Nina's ice cream, but had simply watched Nina eat the poisoned ice cream without warning her, just to avenge himself on Arbenin. Though he tells Arbenin he is his "good genius" (1.1.8), he is not a moral voice introduced to condemn vice, but another of Lermontov's ruthless avengers.

Prince Zvezdich is robbed of his chance to gain revenge and salvage his good name. He had arrived to show Arbenin a letter from Baroness Strahl confessing all. Though the Prince wants to fight a duel with Arbenin, the latter is in no condition to oblige. Thus, although Lermontov rejected Benckendorff's specific recommendation, he did alter the ending drastically. Furthermore, he did so immediately, delaying his departure from St. Petersburg for the purpose. (Mme Arsenieva had been expecting him at Tarkhany since September.) Evidently Lermontov was determined to obtain final approval for his manuscript before leaving the capital. He wrote the fourth act between 8 November and 20 December 1835, and then left for Tarkhany. His close friend Svyatoslav Raevsky agreed to have the new version copied and to submit it to the censorship office.

The second version fared no better with Oldekop than the first. In his report the censor reiterated most of his earlier criticisms, objecting to "unseemly" attacks on the costumed balls at Engelhardt's and to "impertinences directed against ladies of the highest society." Lermontov's negative portrayal of a baroness with a German name quite possibly did not sit well with Oldekop and Benckendorff.

Lermontov was so determined to see his play staged that he revised it a second time, this time totally emasculating it. He substituted an ordinary ball for the masquerade at Engelhardt's, dropped the satirical tone, deleted Baroness Strahl altogether, made Nina actually guilty of infidelity, and had Arbenin only pretend to poison her: afterward he takes the bourgeois path of separation before abandoning society forever.

Even this did not work. The censor was much more impressed, but for reasons unknown withheld his approval. Evidently infidelity and the breakup of a marriage were more than Benckendorff could stomach. Later, in a final act of foolishness, the censorship approved publication of Lermontov's first revision, with some cuts, in 1842—a year after the author's death.

So ended the year-long saga of Lermontov's attempt to have a play performed on the St. Petersburg stage. He had not tried to gain such approval for any of his three previous plays, written during his Moscow years. How are we to explain the extraordinary lengths to which Lermontov went in this case?

The answer, I think, is that Lermontov viewed *The Masquerade* as his path to success in St. Petersburg high society. He hoped to have the play performed at the Imperial Theater, which was attended by members of the highest levels of that society, including the imperial family. The play features a masquerade at Engelhardt's, and it was widely known that these masquerades and balls were attended by the members of the Tsar's family. What greater triumph could the young Lermontov hope to win than the staging of a play about St. Petersburg high society before members of that same society at the Imperial Theater?

Since *The Masquerade* is written not only *about* but *for* St. Petersburg high society, for the first time Lermontov had a specific audience in mind when creating a work. This was a critically new departure for him: in the past he had cared only about himself, even in his love lyrics. Although Lermontov may have been motivated by snobbery and ambition, *The Masquerade* made him a writer aware of his public. When he selected contemporary society as both subject and object of his writing, Lermontov entered into a dialogue with his contemporaries.

End of the Drama

That dialogue, however, was not to be conducted through drama, for Lermontov never wrote a play again. He abandoned a play he started between January and March 1836, while staying at Tarkhany. This prose play was dashed off hastily; the manuscript has no title or list of characters. Later editors have agreed to call the play *Dva brata* [Two Brothers] (3:381–415). It has five acts, but only the final act has more than one scene.

The play's plot, and the names of the characters, are all too familiar. Two brothers, Alexander and Yury, are rivals for the love of Vera Zagorskina, who has recently married Prince Ligov-skoy. Both are unhappy at her happiness, and both speak in highly melodramatic tones about their passions. When Alexander says in act 5 that he is "alone, always alone, cast out like Cain, for God knows whose crime . . . ," Yury could just as well be talking: both recall Byron and Lermontov's earlier heroes. It seems that Lermontov has divided different aspects of himself (or his self-image) between Alexander and Yury.

Alexander is the more dynamic and ruthless of the two: he had had an affair with Vera before her marriage, even while Yury was passionately in love with her. Vera is now anxious to forget both of them, though she admits that she has made a marriage of convenience to a wealthy man. When Alexander demands that she love him again and become his savior, she replies: "I am no angel; I am a weak, foolish woman. I don't understand you . . . I am afraid of you!" (act 2).

The father of the two brothers, who is near death, warns her husband, and he immediately prepares to take Vera away to the country. But this does not prevent tragedy. The brothers quarrel as their father lies on his deathbed. Alexander tells Yury the terrible secret that he was Vera's lover; Yury faints; their father dies; Alexander laments that one cannot trust women or believe in love and virtue.

It is not hard to understand why Lermontov dropped this play. It was less a serious effort at playwriting than a verbalization of his excitement and frustration after seeing Varenka again as he had in December 1835, this time as the wife of another man.

Lermontov's remaining two major works written during his St. Petersburg apprenticeship also demonstrate his growing interest in contemporary high society as a source of material. These are his long comic narrative poem *Sashka* (the hero's name), and another unfinished piece of prose fiction called *Knyaginya Ligovskaya* [Princess Ligovskaya]. Although both works contain many features and characters drawn from earlier writings, on balance they point to the future, marking an important stage in his development: the transition from juvenilia to the works of his mature period. Consequently, both will be discussed later.

By 1836 Lermontov's life had fallen into a familiar pattern. The social whirl was only a gallop away from his quarters with the Life Guard Hussars at Tsarskoe Selo, near the capital, and furthermore he maintained an apartment in St. Petersburg itself. And yet Lermontov did not seem satisfied. It is significant that during 1836 he turned once again—after an interval of four years—to Byron for inspiration. First he translated and adapted a passage from canto 4 of *Childe Harold,* then translated two lyrics: "My soul is dark . . ." (one of Byron's "Hebrew Melodies") and "Lines Written in an Album, at Malta." The latter two poems obviously had special meaning for Lermontov, since he included them in his small collection of poetry published in 1840.

In some mysterious way, while wenching, drinking, and playing soldier at Tsarskoe Selo, Lermontov had become a poet instead of merely a precocious rhymer. But he was searching for something which would help him revive the lyrical impulse that had died after his arrival in St. Petersburg in 1832. This something came suddenly at the end of January 1837, with the senseless death of Alexander Pushkin in a duel.

Chapter Four
Mature Lyrics

Pushkin's Death and Lermontov

Like Byron, the man he so much admired, Lermontov became famous overnight, but in very different circumstances and with very different results. The publication in 1812 of the first two cantos of Byron's *Childe Harold* brought him fame which thereafter spread rapidly throughout Europe. Twenty-five years later Lermontov's poem "Death of a Poet," written in response to Pushkin's death and quickly circulated in manuscript copies, made him both famous and suspect with the authorities.

Pushkin was mortally wounded on 27 January 1837 in a pistol duel with Baron Georges d'Anthès, an exile from France since the July Revolution of 1830 and one of many shabby foreign careerists in the Russian capital, over the honor of Pushkin's wife, Natalya. News of the fatal duel spread throughout the capital within hours. The next day, in a fury, Lermontov wrote his poem; with his consent Svyatoslav Raevsky began to make and distribute copies to friends and acquaintances even before Pushkin's death on 29 January. In the end hundreds, even thousands, of copies came into existence. Lermontov had been in bed for some time with a mysterious ailment, and his condition worsened when he heard of people defending d'Anthès and accusing Pushkin of behaving badly (even his grandmother was against Pushkin).

A week later, Lermontov was visited in his St. Petersburg apartment by a doctor who had been at Pushkin's bedside and recounted to his feverish patient not only the details of his death but the conflicting opinions about the duel. When one of Lermontov's many young relatives repeated the slander against Pushkin, Lermontov dashed off the last sixteen lines of the poem, the ones which caused him most trouble with the authorities, for they accused the court of responsibility for the poet's death. It is not surprising that "Death of a Poet" could not be published in Russia until the reign of a new tsar began.

The poem is a splendid example of indignant rhetoric. In its archaic language it recalls the eighteenth-century ode, and as such it is not typical of Lermontov's poetry as a whole. But Lermontov's approach is very much in character. He portrays Pushkin as the quintessential Romantic figure, a poet of divine gifts living among the frivolous rabble, surrounded by malice and envy. Lermontov professes puzzlement at Pushkin's behavior: why did he not simply ignore these people and go his own way? Lermontov uses the phrase "crown of thorns" to link Pushkin to Jesus Christ, in an obvious attempt to emphasize both the poet's importance to Russia and the heinous nature of the crime. At the same time, Lermontov imagines Pushkin dying "with a vain thirst for revenge," a sentiment which contradicts the Christ image, though one would expect it from Lermontov's vengeful heroes.

Lermontov displays patriotic feelings in "Death of a Poet," defending Russian honor against French attack. In the final sixteen lines, however, Lermontov lashed out at the court, if not at the person of the Tsar himself, and threatened them with divine retribution:

> You, standing around the throne in a greedy crowd,
> Butchers of Freedom, Genius and Glory!
> You hide behind the protection of the law;
> Before you are judgment and truth . . . you say nothing!
> But there is also God's judgment, confidants of depravity!
> There is a terrible judgment: it awaits you. (1:373–74)

The epigraph, taken, ironically enough, from an obscure French tragedy in a translation by Lermontov's former tutor, begs the Tsar to enforce justice and punish the murderer. It seems reasonable to assume that the epigraph was added later in a perfectly understandable effort on Lermontov's part to soften the impact of the poem's last sixteen lines: "God's judgment" *(bozhy sud)* and the "terrible judgment" *(grozny sud)* which Lermontov calls down upon the court are echoed by a phrase addressed to the Tsar in the epigraph: "Your righteous judgment" *(Tvoy pravy sud)*.

Pushkin's death was truly a tragic event in the history of Russian literature, but it also revived Lermontov's lyrical impulse and shook him out of his hollow existence as a Hussar. Immediately after the storm broke over his head, Lermontov responded to the emotional intensity of the situation by writing lyrics. After his arrest, Lermontov was confined in a room on the top floor of the General Staff Building. While there, according to Shan-Girey, he wrote a number of lyrics with wine, soot, and matchsticks on bread that he had ordered his servant to roll out to serve as paper. Thus "Death of a Poet," though itself not a great poem, marked the beginning of Lermontov's literary maturity.

The Mature Lyrics

From February 1837 until his death in July 1841 Lermontov wrote more than eighty lyrics, short epistles, and album pieces (I exclude epigrams). More than half of these were produced in the last eighteen months of his life. His output dropped considerably during most of 1838–39, when he was writing his novel, but this is still impressive evidence of the revival of Lermontov's lyric impulse. Moreover, his poetry was of consistently high quality.

Lermontov's exile to the Caucasus proved a blessing in disguise. The marvelous scenery, the exciting people he met, and the new impressions he formed all helped to maintain his artistic excitement. He continued to write lyrics and to take up old projects with fresh insight, including most especially his narrative poem *The Demon*. At Taman he had the experiences that lay behind the story "Taman," part of his novel *A Hero of Our Time*.

The most obvious characteristic of Lermontov's lyrics is their musicality. They are lyrics in the original sense of the term. In Classical times there were three major types of literary work: the narrative, the drama, and the lyric. The lyric was designed to be sung to the accompaniment of a stringed instrument, the lyre. The traditional view of the historical development of the lyric is that, once poems ceased to be sung, meter became a substitute for melody.

Lermontov is generally recognized as the most musical poet in Russian literature. Many of his poems have been set to music, and Anton Rubinstein composed an opera based upon *The Demon*. The melodic quality of many passages in both *The Demon* and *The Novice* is such that it mesmerizes the reader into overlooking the poems' weaknesses of characterization and structure.

Whatever his subject, Lermontov remains first and foremost a lyric poet, even in his narrative poems. We recall that Lermontov was a skilled musician and a talented singer, and that musical ability contributed to the melodic quality of his verse. He freely endowed his characters with his own love of music and sense of its power over human emotions. All Lermontov's heroines sing beautifully, and all his heroes are captivated by the haunting songs they sing. The young novice is charmed by the song of a Georgian girl, and later, in a delirious dream, is enchanted by the singing of a fish with golden scales. The Demon forgets his evil ways, briefly, when he hears Tamara singing and sees her dancing. Even Pechorin is powerfully affected by the Circassian princess Bela's song, and long after he had met her he remembered the song of the "undine" who nearly proved his undoing in "Taman."[1]

It is now generally agreed that Lermontov's chief mentor in the creation of melodious lines was not Pushkin, as many used to think, but Vasily Zhukovsky. Lermontov carefully noted particularly felicitous phrases and sound combinations from Zhukovsky and other poets. And he repeats favorite turns of phrase from one work to another, especially in his juvenilia.

Lermontov used all prosodic features available to him to increase the musicality of his poetry, and did not limit himself to such familiar devices as alliteration, assonance, and onomatopoeia. He experimented to a far greater degree than did Pushkin, and he employed a far wider range of meters. Fully two-thirds of the lines Pushkin wrote are iambic tetrameter, which is also the standard for all nineteenth-century Russian poetry. Lermontov made extensive use of the four-foot iamb, but he avoided feminine rhymes and also introduced a caesura, or pause, after the second foot, i.e., the fourth syllable, which is usually stressed in his usage.

The most striking metrical difference between Lermontov and Pushkin is Lermontov's extensive use of trochees, and of ternary meters, most commonly amphibrachs, in which the middle syllable bears the stress. These meters were rarely used by Russian poets, but Lermontov wrote some of his most famous poems in trochees, amphibrachs, and dactyls. Moreover, in the ternary meters, Lermontov sometimes alternates lines of varying length, e.g., three-foot lines and five-foot lines. He is so adept at handling these difficult technical problems that his poems seem to be phrased quite naturally, even colloquially.

In a brilliant but neglected article published in 1914 the Russian critic Vladimir Fisher pointed out how difficult it is to categorize Lermontov's lyrics by genre or type:

Of the usual types of lyric poetry least well represented in his verse are the ode and satire; and there are no friendly or drinking songs. All the remaining types of lyric poetry are so mixed up that any attempt at sub-grouping would be superfluous: any given poem is at one and the same time a song, a romance, a ballad, an elegy, often a satire, an anthology piece, and an epistle.

Fisher suggested a possible tripartite classification of the lyrics and short poems:

One can only observe that in some poems he expresses himself *directly* [*neposredstvenno*], in others *indirectly* [*posredstvenno*], i.e., by means of symbols and allegory, and in still other poems *incidentally* [*sluchayno*] or apropos. This manner of grouping is important since Lermontov may write a piece that is lyrical from beginning to end and yet not use the pronoun "I" once; Lermontov can be equally lyrical when speaking through another persona, or describing a scene, or telling a story. Lermontov created a special type of lyrical poem, which has the form of a story, but which under no circumstances can be categorized as narrative in spirit.[2]

Fisher's argument may be summarized as follows:

1. Lermontov ignores generic distinctions and incorporates various genre styles and motifs into one and the same poem.

2. Unlike Pushkin, Lermontov does not permit his material to interact naturally with his verbal form: "With Lermontov we find great stability of imagery and phrasing, but instability in subjects."

3. Whatever their ostensible topic, Lermontov's lyrics all focus upon the poet's personal feelings and/or thoughts.

4. Lermontov created a special kind of poem which has the "form of a story" *(forma povestvovaniya)* but still is a lyric, not a narrative poem. In fact, these poems represent the "quintessence of feeling."

5. Lermontov is an Impressionist poet; he uses both symbolism and allegory, but always to express his own feelings and/or thoughts.

6. It is most reasonable to classify Lermontov's lyrics according to the intensity and "directness" of the personal expression. Fisher suggests a tripartite division.

Boris Eykhenbaum incorporated several of these notions in the section on Lermontov in his *Melodika russkogo liricheskogo stikha* [Melodic Features in the Russian Lyric, 1922] and in his famous study of Lermontov published in 1924. Eykhenbaum praises Fisher's article in general terms in a footnote on the first page of the latter book as a unique attempt to "return to the concrete analysis of Lermontov's style." He then mentions Fisher in one other footnote at the end of his book when acknowledging his debt to Fisher's idea that Lermontov was concerned with finding a place for his favorite turns of phrase rather than with the demands of the material at hand.

But Eykhenbaum's indebtedness to Vladimir Fisher's article is far more profound than this. Eykhenbaum takes from Fisher a number of his central theses about Lermontov's works which have become standard in all later scholarship: first, the notion

of Lermontov's "art of fusion" (*iskusstvo splava*); second, the idea
of what he calls "poems with a plot" (*syuzhetnye stikhi*) or "lyric
with a plot" (*syuzhetnaya lirika*); and third, his stress on the
"meditative" nature of Lermontov's lyrics. Eykhenbaum divides
Lermontov's poems into types he designates as "oratorical and
plotted romance lyrics" (*oratorskaya i syuzhetnoromansnaya lirika*).

I will base my discussion of Lermontov's mature lyrics upon
Fisher's tripartite classification. Since Fisher himself simply lists
the poems, usually without comment, I shall provide my own
analyses of individual poems within Fisher's categories.

The first thing to be said about the categories is that they have
fluid boundaries. Moreover, the number of poems in the first
category (direct expression) is very large; in the second (indirect
expression), somewhat smaller; and in the third (incidental
expression), quite small. In fact, Fisher found it necessary to
subdivide his first category into three subsets:

(i)   attitudes toward "God, eternity, nature, people, life
       and death";
(ii)   attitudes toward "political events, the nation and so-
       ciety, literature, and his own poetic activity";
(iii) love lyrics.

If we examine Lermontov's poems of 1837, the first year of
his mature period, we will see how they fit into the categories
and subsets outlined above. Wherever possible, I discuss lyrics
which are reworkings of poems from his apprenticeship years
(1828–32), so as to show by concrete example Lermontov's new
mastery of his craft. For the most part, Lermontov expresses the
same feelings and thoughts in his mature period as he had previously. But now they are carried in vessels of gemlike hardness
and brilliance.

Lyricism and Philosophy

Lermontov wrote at least four poems while confined after his
arrest in 1837. It is also possible that he either wrote or revised
his famous poem "Borodino" at about this time. The four

poems—listed by Shan-Girey in his memoirs—are "Uznik" [The Captive], "Sosed" [The Neighbor], "Kogda volnuetsya zhelte-yushchaya niva" [When the Ripening Corn Waves Golden], and "Molitva" [A Prayer] (*Vosp.*, 43). They obviously had some importance for Lermontov, for he included them in his 1840 collection.

Fisher puts the latter two poems, which have become very popular, into subset one of his first category, as leading representatives of the lyric which expresses directly, without symbol and allegory, Lermontov's attitude toward "God, eternity, nature, people, life and death." To call these views "philosophy" is to load the poems with more systematic intellectual freight than they can carry. In some of his later essays Eykhenbaum exaggerates the philosophical content of Lermontov's poems and goes source-hunting in the works of Schelling, Schiller, and other German estheticians and philosophers.[3] The fact is that such ideas as the intimate relationship between good and evil were "in the air" at the time, and Lermontov could have picked them up from Byron, Shakespeare, or any one of a dozen other poets.

Fisher too speaks of "philosophy," but with the qualification that "the poet expresses his philosophy so picturesquely and so emotionally that it does not weaken the poetry." This is a more subtle understanding of the relationship among thought, feeling, and poetic art in the poems.

"When the Ripening Corn Waves Golden" consists of four quatrains written in iambs, mostly hexameter, but some pentameter and tetrameter.[4] The rhyme scheme is aBaB. The first three stanzas begin with "When," and the first two lines of the last stanza with "Then." The poem is therefore structured as one long sentence, and has been taught in Russian schools, as an example of logical sentence structure.[5]

The work is pure pantheism, recalling many of William Wordsworth's poems. Its general point is that the sights, sounds, and smells of nature inspire the poet and make him forget his troubles:

> And I can achieve happiness on earth,
> And in the heavens I see God . . .

Stanza one contains essentially a description of late summer, stanza two of spring (the lily of the valley blooms in May), and stanza three is something of a puzzle, for the "freezing cold spring" *(studyony klyuch)* mentioned need point to no particular season of the year. The important element in the third stanza is the intensification of the communication between nature and the poet, suggested in the second stanza by the image of the lily of the valley nodding "affably" to him. The lyrical "I" is introduced by implication in the second line, then directly in the third. Furthermore, the spring speaks to the poet of the "peaceful realm" from which it has come. The use in the third stanza of such emotionally charged phrases as "vague dream," "mysterious saga," and "peaceful realm" surely signals a forward movement, preparing us for the resolution in the final stanza. The semantic and emotional logic of the poem should be clear, though it does not rule out other sequences, such as those of tone or intonation.

As its title suggests, "A Prayer" is also a religious poem. The poet addresses the Virgin Mary to pray for the happiness of an innocent maid in this life, asking that at her death an angel be sent to bear up her "beautiful soul." The poem contains obvious echoes of Lermontov's early lyric "The Angel." In that poem, however, the poet emphasizes the plight of the innocent soul on earth, while here he focuses on the return to heaven after a brief, but possibly joyful, worldly existence.

"A Prayer" has a remarkably complex rhythm. It is written in four-foot dactyls, varied on occasion when the stress falls outside the established pattern. The opening line provides a good example of this:

> Yá, Máter Bózhiya, nýne s molítvoyu.
> (I, Mother of God, now with a prayer)

Strictly speaking, the first and second syllables should not both be stressed, though the second stress is deemphasized by the sense of the line. Another example, this time beginning with an anapest rather than a dactyl, is:

> Okruzhí schástiem dúshu dostóynuyu
> (Surround her worthy soul with happiness),

or again:

> Tý vospriyát poshlí k lózhu pechálnomu
> (Send to the sad couch to receive her).

where *poshli* should bear no stress, according to the meter. We forgive Lermontov these irregularities because in reading the poem aloud we are carried along by the rhythm and the meaning as he demonstrates his complete mastery in the creative union of rhythm and sense.

The dactylic rhyming (abab) is also brilliant. In English verse dactylic endings to lines usually occur in comic poems because they fit jingles. In Russian folklore they are standard, but it is still difficult to use them convincingly in Russian "high" poetry.

"A Prayer" is structured on a "Not . . . but . . ." sequence. The poet first says he is not praying for himself, then states his real purpose in the middle of the second stanza. He speaks of his "deserted soul" and calls himself a "wanderer" by which he means an "exile." The poet also expresses his own feelings about life with a reference to the "cold world."

Subset two of the first category is represented in 1837 by "Death of a Poet," which has already been discussed. This poem expresses very directly Lermontov's attitudes toward "political events, the nation and society, literature, and his own poetic activity." In fact, I would argue that in venting his rage over Pushkin's fate, Lermontov was at the same time speaking of his own predicament in society both as a poet and as an individual. But "Death of a Poet" may also be placed in category three (as it is by Fisher) since it was written for a specific occasion and Lermontov expressed his feelings "incidentally."

Lermontov's eight-line poem "Rasstalis my, no tvoy portret" [We Have Parted, But Your Portrait] belongs to subset three, the love lyrics. Fisher makes an interesting comparison with the love lyrics of Byron, who introduced the emotion-laden poem in which the poet mentions a single painful incident in a love affair, and then obliges the reader to imagine for himself "some complex emotional drama experienced by the poet," or even "a whole life of suffering and passion."

The problem with this type of poem is that it takes a delicate touch to avoid crossing the line between creative hint and irritating mystification. In his early love lyrics Lermontov was all too often rather heavy-handed.

"We Have Parted" is based on an eight-line poem of 1831 that Lermontov wrote in Ekaterina Sushkova's album, beginning "Ya ne lyublyu tebya . . ." [I do not love you . . .]. The early poem is too abstract; it speaks of "torments" and an "image," whereas the revised version refers to a specific portrait which the poet carries against his breast. Furthermore, the vague "previous dream" of the early poem now becomes the "pale ghost" of the poet's best days, associated directly with the portrait.

In the 1831 poem Lermontov was too specific about the poet's current feelings, and so the seventh line, "I still could not forget it" (the image), is puzzling, while at the same time the background details are too vague. In the 1837 version, Lermontov reverses his approach, defining the details more sharply and leaving the poet's feelings more ambiguous. This change also tightens the poem's structure, since it proceeds logically from the separation of the lovers (why did they part?) to the poet's ambivalent feelings of regret (he still loves the beloved's portrait, but does he still love her?). The last two lines merely hint at answers:

> Thus an abandoned temple is still a temple,
> An idol cast down is still a god![6]

The category of indirect expression "by means of symbolic images and allegories" is represented by "The Captive" and "The Neighbor." As an illustration I will discuss "The Captive." In 1832 Lermontov had written a poem entitled "Zhelanie" [Desire] beginning with the same four lines as "The Captive." He retained only those lines from the earlier poem, which had consisted of three stanzas of nine lines each (aBaBcDccD). The new poem preserves the trochaic tetrameter, and also consists of three stanzas, but they have eight lines each (aBaBccDD). This tightening of the rhyme scheme is reinforced by the particularizing of the detail.

If in the earlier poem Lermontov had moved on from his opening motifs—a horse and a black-eyed beauty—to vague talk of boats, storms, palaces, and gardens, now he develops the original images. In the second four lines of the first stanza the captive tells us he will kiss the girl and ride the steed into the steppe. The second stanza begins with a "but": he recognizes that his prison is too strong; he pictures the beauty and the horse outside, beyond his reach. The third stanza returns him to the loneliness of captivity, as he forgets his dream of escape:

> All I can hear behind the door [of my cell]
> Is the regular sound of footsteps,
> As in the midnight silence
> The wordless sentry walks his rounds.

Ending with the image of the "wordless" and presumably indifferent sentry provides a broader framework for the captive's fond dreams, as Lermontov achieves a marvelous balance between particular detail and universal tone. The author gives validity to the world beyond the hero's own desires with just a slight hint of irony. In his apprenticeship years Lermontov scarcely ever had his lyrical hero conceive a dream and then recognize its impossibility calmly and sadly.

In this poem Lermontov also demonstrates complete mastery of meter and rhyme. He emphasizes the singing rhythm of trochees by the frequent use of four- and five-syllable words at the beginnings of lines.

"The Captive" treats an enduring Romantic motif: that of the poet trapped in an unkind world from which there is no escape, except through the imagination. The poet knows there exists a purer, more divine existence, but he can never attain it: hence the pessimistic frustration of the idealistic Byronic hero.

"Borodino"

The third category, that of incidental expression, includes pieces written for or as a result of a special occasion, as well as epistles, album verses, and epigrams. A good illustration of such poems for 1837 is the famous "Borodino," which Fisher does not categorize. It was written in response to the patriotic excitement aroused by the twenty-fifth anniversary of the great battle in which the Russians under Kutuzov fought Napoleon to a standstill just west of Moscow. Both sides suffered tremendous casualties, but the Russians withdrew and the French occupied Moscow shortly afterward. The French, who call this engagement the Battle of the Moscow River, count it a victory, but the Russians were proud of their stout resistance.

We do not know exactly when Lermontov wrote this poem, but it seems reasonable to suppose that he used it as a counterweight to "Death of a Poet." Raevsky did not mention it in his official statement to the authorities, whereas he did refer to a poem of 1835, "Opyat, narodnye vitii" [Again, Popular Orators], a jingoistic attack on the French press for urging Polish liberation from Russian domination. Even if Lermontov had written "Borodino" before "Death of a Poet," he quickly saw the wisdom of getting it into print as fast as possible. With uncharacteristic haste he arranged to have it published in the June 1837 issue of *Sovremennik*, a journal founded by Pushkin the previous year.

Once again Lermontov took an earlier poem as the basis for a new work. In "Pole Borodino" [The Field of Borodino, 1830–31], a poem of six stanzas of eleven lines each, Lermontov presented an eyewitness account of the battle by a participant. The poem does not work because the narrator is not particularized and uses an artificial style. It is not clear whom he is addressing and why he is telling his story. In the course of the poem the narrator mentions a friend who dies, but the friend remains as faceless as the narrator himself. The poem lacks structure and movement.

In "Borodino" the narrative is framed and the speaker is particularized. He is an old soldier describing the battle to some young upstarts and explaining why the Russians abandoned Moscow to the French. Its language is appropriately salty, unlike the "poetic" diction of the earlier poem. The nameless soldier is only too glad to "tell it like it was," not sparing the feelings of his audience: he bluntly contrasts his courageous dead brethren with "today's crowd." The crusty old-timer's contempt for the younger generation is psychologically valid, and also reflects an important motif in Lermontov's works: the condemnation of contemporary society and the "heroes of the time." This brief but pointed link between past and present also tightens the poem's structure.

Lermontov makes another improvement by dropping the first four lines of the clumsy, shapeless eleven-line stanza of the earlier poem while retaining the metrics and rhyming scheme of the remaining seven: aaBcccB. The strong masculine rhymes of lines 3 and 7, which are trimeters instead of tetrameters, tighten the new stanza. Another structural device, a favorite of Lermontov's, helps round the poem off naturally. The old soldier's opening stanza—praising the men of his time, regretting their harsh fate, and insisting that only God's will obliged the Russians to leave Moscow to the invader—recurs at the close with a change in the second line, which, instead of "today's crowd," refers to "a powerful, dashing bunch of guys." This change underscores the heroic qualities of the older generation as Lermontov punches his message home.

Perhaps the most significant development in this poem was Lermontov's choice as narrator of a character totally unlike himself in birth, education, social class, attitudes, age, and experience. The poem is a monologue, like so much of Lermontov's work, but here for the first time he manages to step outside himself. The old soldier as a stylized narrator foreshadows Maksim Maksimych in *A Hero of Our Time,* as well as the singer and indeed all the characters of Lermontov's brilliant adaptation of the old Russian "historical tale" about the Merchant Kalashnikov, set in the times of Ivan the Terrible.

Lyrics of the Second Exile

It would be pressing the point to insist that Lermontov's second exile to the Caucasus was a blessing, disguised or not. During the two years he had spent in St. Petersburg after his first exile, he had composed remarkable works in both prose and verse, including some fine lyrics. But it is undeniable that he wrote many of his most enduring lyric poems in the last year of his life, while in the Caucasus or on his travels.

Among the lyrics Lermontov wrote in 1838 were his beautiful "Kazachya kolybelnaya pesnya" [Cossack Cradle Song], which was later set to music and rocked countless babies to sleep in Russia; three short poems expressing admiration for the voice of a female singer, probably Praskovya Barteneva, whom he met frequently at the Karamzins' soirees: "Slyshu li golos tvoy" [Whenever I Hear Your Voice], "Kak nebesa, tvoy vzor blistaet" [Like the Heavens, Your Gaze Is Radiant], and "Ona poyot—i zvuki tayut" [She Sings—and the Sounds Melt]; and "Poet" [The Poet]. In this last poem the narrator tells the exciting story of his dagger, now abandoned and useless, then addresses a poet to ask:

> In our pampered age have you too, poet,
> Not lost your purpose;
> Having exchanged for gold the power which society
> Used to listen to in mute reverence?

"The Poet" deals with a traditional theme of the Romantic period, but in an interesting way. The poem is written from the viewpoint of one who regrets that the poet cannot, or will not, play a more vital role in the life of society.

Among Lermontov's lyrics of 1839 the most noteworthy are a charming poem addressed to the infant son of his friend Aleksey Lopukhin, "Rebyonka milogo rozhdenie" [The Birth of a Sweet Baby]; "Ne ver sebe" [Do Not Trust Yourself], which contradicts the view of "The Poet" and advises the "young dreamer" to keep all his bitterness and grief to himself, because the crowd is indifferent to them; and two remarkable lyrical allegories: "Tri palmy" [Three Palms] and "Dary Tereka" [Gifts of the Terek River].[7]

"Three Palms" is subtitled "An Eastern Legend." Along with "Gifts of the Terek" it belongs to that group of poems with the "form of a story" which remain essentially lyrical. "Three Palms" tells the story of an oasis which is enjoyed by an Arab caravan, whose members cut the palms down to make logs for a fire in the evening. Henceforth there is no shade and no spring, only parched desert. At the beginning of the poem the palm trees had complained to God that they had no purpose in life: "We have grown and flourished in the desert without benefit to anyone." Too late they realize God's design.

Among the few lyrics Lermontov wrote in the early months of 1840 before departing for the Caucasus we find one of his most brilliant love poems, "Rebyonku" [To a Child]. As Fisher maintains, this is a perfect example of a poem containing the veiled hint in the Byronic manner. It begins in traditional fashion, but then the poet asks the child if his mother ("she") has mentioned any other name when they said their prayers together; the poet tells the child to forget the name, but if he should recall it, then not to curse it. Underlying the lyric is a complex set of relationships and a tragedy whose memory must be suppressed by both the man and the woman.

Fisher assigns another poem, addressed to Princess Maria Shcherbatova, a beautiful young widow with whom Lermontov may have been in love, to his third category of incidental expression rather than to the love lyrics, because it is an occasional piece. It might also be placed in the second category (indirect expression), since the beloved becomes a symbol of an innocent existence from another world.

In January 1840 Lermontov wrote and published one of his most famous lyrics, "I skuchno i grustno" [I Am Bored and Sad]. This poem again demonstrates Lermontov's extraordinary facility with ternary meters. The three quatrains are written in amphibrachs, with the first and third lines having five feet, the second line three feet, and the fourth line four feet. The rhyming is AbAb. Lermontov achieves an amazing unity between metric rhythm and word boundaries in this poem, while at the same time his language is conversational and natural, as though the poet were talking either to himself or with a friend who now and then takes issue with his totally gloomy view of human existence. The poet makes an opening statement, then goes on to consider ways to make life interesting and exciting—desires, love, passions—only to conclude:

> And life, when you look around with cold attention,
> Is an empty and stupid joke. . . .

In spite of the poem's difficult meter and lengthy lines, Lermontov varies the rhythm by introducing pauses after questions and using phrases of different length, from quick exclamations to statements occupying almost a whole line.

Lermontov wrote his famous poem "Tuchi" [Clouds] on the eve of his departure for the Caucasus in early May 1840. The Karamzins had arranged a farewell party for him, in a show of kindness which appeared to touch the poet. After looking out the window for some time, he recited the poem, which greatly affected his hearers.

One can only marvel again at Lermontov's technical skill. The poem consists of three stanzas, written in four-foot dactyls with alternating rhymes. Once more he shows absolute mastery in matching rhythm and meaning, specifically words with metric feet. The opening line may serve as an example:

> Túchki nebésnye, véchnye stránniki!
> (Heavenly clouds, eternal wanderers!)

In the opening stanza the poet describes the clouds and compares them to himself as a wanderer from north to south. In the second stanza he asks about the reasons for the clouds' southward movement in a series of rhetorical questions. Then, in the third stanza, he discounts the reasons suggested:

> No, you are bored with barren cornfields . . .
> Passions are alien to you, and alien is suffering;

> Eternally cold, eternally free,
> You have no homeland, you are not exiles.

The poet starts to link himself with the clouds, then pulls back. Clouds are not people; they can have no feelings. At the same time, the last stanza implies that the poet longs to be like the clouds, even if they do not resemble him.

Among the more than two dozen poems Lermontov wrote in the last year of his life are two about his attitude toward Russia. The first, "Rodina" [My Homeland], expresses his irrational love of Russia and its life, chiefly its natural beauties and popular holidays (not its cities and high society!). The second is a short poem which begins:

> Farewell, unwashed Russia,
> Land of slaves, land of lords,
> And you, pale blue uniforms,
> And you, nation devoted to them.

The blue uniforms are those of the secret police of the Third Section (and of the KGB today). Lermontov's disgust at the Russian people's slave mentality is echoed in a remark he made in early 1841 to Yury Samarin (in French): "What is worse is not that a certain number of men suffer patiently, but that an enormous number suffer without even knowing it." (*Vosp.*, 297).

Another poem, "Utyos" [The Rock], again employs one of Lermontov's favorite symbols, clouds. It is written in the very rare trochaic pentameter with feminine rhyme (abba) throughout, also very rare. The poem consists of only two quatrains which tell a touching story. Using the past tense, the poet describes a "golden cloud" that rests for the night against a rock, then departs the following morning. Only dew remains from the cloud as the old rock is left alone again:

> Solitary
> It stands, plunged in deep thought,
> And quietly weeps in the wilderness.

The rock obviously symbolizes the isolated poet, so typical of the Romantic era. But the first-person pronoun does not occur, and the poet does not intrude into his poem. The cloud is free, and indifferent to the problems of this earth.

In general, the lyrics Lermontov wrote toward the end of his life are pessimistic. Naturally, Lermontov was not downcast at all times, and one cannot judge a poet's mood by any one lyric poem. The constant repetition of gloomy thoughts, however, probably suggests Lermontov's doubts about his future and regrets about his present. One of his most famous poems, written in the last weeks of his life, is "Vykhozhu odin ya na dorogu" [I Walk Out Alone onto the Road]. The poem consists of five quatrains in trochaic pentameters, but the rhythm is often iambic because lines begin with an unstressed first syllable. The rhyming is aBaB. The poet describes a quiet, starlit night when "the desert harkens unto God,/And star speaks with star" as the earth "sleeps in blue radiance." Yet the poet is troubled. He no longer expects anything from life; he wishes only that he could enter an eternal state of suspended animation:

> So that all night and all day caressing my ears,
> A sweet voice would sing of love,
> So that above me with leaves forever green
> A dark oak would bend and rustle.

The poet seeks, not death—he says he does not wish to sleep "the cold sleep of the grave"—but rather an oblivion akin to total indifference.

Even the love of women has lost its appeal for Lermontov's lyrical hero. Now he is more likely to recall past passions than to celebrate emotions in the present. So for example, in "Net, ne tebya tak pylko ya lyublyu" [No, It Is Not You I Love So Ardently] the poet tells his beloved that when they converse, his heart is talking "with the friend of my youthful days" all the while. At the end of the poem we learn that his earlier beloved is now dead.

The theme of death recurs frequently in Lermontov's last year. "A Dream" is one of several poems in which Lermontov, or his lyrical hero, imagines his own death. The poet envisions his body lying in a valley of Daghestan, bleeding from a bullet wound in the chest. Only at the end of the second stanza do we learn that he is sleeping "the sleep of the dead." In the third stanza the dead poet dreams of a gay party in his homeland at which young women speak of him. He sees that one of the girls does not participate in the conversation:

> And her young soul into a sorrowful dream
> Was plunged by God knows what.

In the fifth stanza this girl herself has a dream in which she sees "the corpse of one known to her" lying in the valley of Daghestan. Certain phrases are repeated from the opening stanza as Lermontov closes the poem with the annular device, returning to the beginning, a favorite technique of his. Although he never says so, the poet is himself dreaming at the outset, so that the poem contains three dreams, one inside the other like a Matryoshka doll.

The frequency with which Lermontov treated the theme of death at this time is hardly surprising. He was, after all, engaged in quite active fighting. He displayed great bravery in battle, and twice was recommended for decorations, though St. Petersburg declined to grant them. He saw death all around him. Lermontov contemplated his own death poetically, but this does not mean at all that he had a death wish.

We may, however, reasonably infer from the evidence of his poems that Lermontov saw himself as isolated from the mass of the population, ridiculed by fashionable society, and distrusted by the benighted government and its minions. This sense of isolation comes through clearly in "Prorok" [The Prophet], which recalls Pushkin's famous poem of the same name. Pushkin had felt just as Lermontov did about his position in Russia.

Four years previously, Lermontov had burst onto the social and literary scene as a result of Pushkin's death in a duel. He quickly broke out of his Byronic chrysalis into mature poetry and prose. Sadly, he did not handle his personal and public life with much finesse. It is clear that he was desperately and genuinely unhappy.

Chapter Five
Narrative Poems

Traditionally, Lermontov's two most famous narrative poems have been *The Novice* and *The Demon*.[1] Both belong to the most Byronic portion of the Lermontov canon and offer quintessential examples of the Byronic hero. Precisely these qualities made the works so popular throughout the nineteenth century, but twentieth-century readers have generally valued them less highly. In much the same way, the popularity of Byron's most "Byronic" works (*Lara, The Corsair*) has declined, while his ironical and satiric poems, especially *Don Juan* and *Beppo,* have gained in public favor.

Although *The Novice* and *The Demon* were completed only toward the end of Lermontov's life, they had been begun near the outset of his brief career. They therefore pose a problem for those who argue that there is a linear development from Romanticism to Realism (however defined) in Lermontov's works. They are out of phase chronologically because they look back to his early Byronic period and yet were finished at a time when he was writing his novel, *A Hero of Our Time,* which contains a critique of the Byronic type. Where then does one place these works in Lermontov's development in view of the fact that he tinkered with various drafts of them (particularly *The Demon*) throughout the 1830s? I shall discuss them first, because they represent nothing new: they merely close down the Romantic, Byronic poem as a creative mode. I believe Lermontov sensed this, but wanted to complete them by way of purging himself of certain notions and attitudes he had cherished earlier.

The Novice

The Novice was written in 1839, but draws heavily on two earlier unpublished poems, *Ispoved* [The Confession, 1831] and

Boyarin Orsha [The Boyar Orsha, 1835–36]. *The Demon,* first outlined in 1829, went through seven revisions in the following decade. Lermontov's exile to the Caucasus in 1837 helped crystallize the original concepts behind both works, and he found in the scenic grandeur of the Caucasus the ideal setting for each.

The basic narrative of *The Novice* derives from a story told to Lermontov in 1837 at the Mtskheti Monastery in Tbilisi by an old monk who had spent his entire life at the monastery after being brought there as a foundling. Lermontov chose to make his hero, the novice, more defiant. Instead of passively living out his life in the monastery, he dies at the conclusion after a frustrated but passionately exciting attempt to escape to his native region in the Caucasus mountains.

He asks the monk to bury him in the monastery garden within sight of his beloved mountains:

> And with that thought I shall fall asleep
> And will not curse anyone.

The novice's dying hope that a brother or friend will wipe the sweat from his brow is rather touching. The French scholar Eugène Duchesne has suggested that this calm, though not truly resigned, attitude reflected a mellowing in Lermontov's own views toward the end of the 1830s.[2]

The Novice demonstrates Lermontov's weakness in handling narrative stance, something he acquired from Byron. This poem consists of an extended monologue spoken to the old monk, so that no dialogue occurs between the characters. The old monk remains silent and, to us, nearly invisible. At the opening of two sections, the novice asks the old monk directly: "Do you want to know what I saw while I was free?" (section 6), and "Do you want to know what I did while I was free?" (section 8). There is no reply; we must assume that the old man simply gives wordless assent. This accentuates the monologic quality of Lermontov's narrative poems. We have noted this same weakness in his attempts at writing drama. Lermontov, a Romantic and a lyricist, is concerned only with the speaker's feelings, not the reactions of the listener.

A further narrative shortcoming is that Lermontov sets the scene for the novice's confession in two opening sections, spoken by a nameless narrator. This narrator is not particularized in any way, and he disappears for good after making this introduction. But what he tells us is important: the novice had been brought as a frightened native boy to the monastery by a Russian general. A kindly monk takes care of him and gains his trust, so that he seems to grow up normally. He even takes vows and prepares to enter the priesthood. Then one fall day he suddenly disappears, to be found three days later exhausted and near death. He is brought back to the monastery and the old monk arrives to administer the last rites, whereupon the novice proudly delivers the confession which forms the remainder of the poem. It is part apologia, part complaint, part paean to the beauties of the Caucasus.

The novice is most distressed at dying so young, before he had had a chance to experience life's joys and sorrows. Even his childhood had been stolen from him, for he had never heard "those holy words: father and mother." He describes himself in the monastery as "in soul a child, by fate a monk," and says in section 14 that he escaped in an attempt to return home, to recapture the childhood he had been denied:

> . . . Only one aim,
> To reach my native land,
> Did I have in my soul.

He recalls his home in section 6, though in vague, if rhapsodic language. The novice does remember a real home, a real place, but what he is searching for now is less a physical place than an idealized Golden Age. Thus the poem describes a symbolic search, an attempt to escape the trials of earthly existence. The novice's lack of success supports this symbolic interpretation. Lermontov's view of life was pessimistic; many of his other works embody his belief that life was merely "a vale of tears." Only the love of women and the scenic beauties of nature might offer momentary joy, but this soon passes, too.

The Novice contains an extended treatment of themes broached in two famous early lyrics, "The Sail" and "The Angel." The novice's character recalls the rebellious nature of the personified sail which "seeks the storm, /As though calm could be found in storms." The novice speaks of his "raging" and "tormented" breast in sections 4 and 9, and in section 8 he cries out:

> . . . Oh, like a brother
> I would be glad to embrace the storm!
> I would follow the clouds with my eyes,
> And reach for the stars.

A few lines later he speaks of "That friendship, brief but alive, / Between a turbulent heart and a storm."

The highlights of his wanderings are (1) the sight of a lovely Georgian girl descending to fill her jug with water from a clear stream, and the sounds of her beautiful song; (2) his fight with a leopard which he kills with a wooden club; (3) a delirious dream in which he imagines he is lying happily at the bottom of a cool, deep stream, listening to a song sung in a silvery voice by a beautiful golden fish with tender green eyes.

In typically Romantic fashion, Lermontov emphasized the divine quality of music. Two of the three episodes mentioned above involve a beautiful song, which symbolizes, as in "The Angel," a link between earthly existence and the Paradise from which we have fallen (in Christian terms), or else some neo-Platonic ideal reality behind the vulgar, physical reality surrounding us.

The novice observes the Georgian girl without meeting her. The hero's overwhelming concern is to get back home; during his wanderings he chiefly enjoys his freedom and the beauties of nature. He achieves such a unity with the natural world that in his fight with the leopard he becomes an animal, while the leopard takes on human features.

Like many other Lermontovian heroes, the novice believes fate is against him. He struggles to achieve his goal, but there is an element of fatalism within him: "But in vain did I quarrel with fate, / It mocked me!" A little later, in section 20, he declares that he deserves his fate: even a horse can make its way back home, but he could not. Then he compares himself at length with a flower grown in a dark dungeon: when first brought out into the bright sun the flower rejoices, but all too soon it fades and dies, unaccustomed to the light.

The Novice contains some remarkably fine lines in the hero's impassioned descriptions of the exotic scenery that he had seen close at hand for the first time in his adult life. But these descriptions resemble set pieces, linked together only tangentially by the person of the hero and his aimless wandering. He talks to no one. The novice simply talks and the reader, like the poor old monk, is obliged to listen to his constant complaints.

The Demon

Like the novice, Lermontov's Demon finds he cannot go home again either, and also fails to escape his fate. The Demon sees in a beautiful Georgian princess the same mirage of happiness that the novice does in the magnificent Caucasus mountains. Flying above the earth, the Demon glimpses the lovely Tamara, who arouses him from his cosmic boredom and disgust with everything human. In order to attain everlasting joy with her, the Demon has her bridegroom killed by bandits on the way to the wedding, and then lays siege to her heart and soul. Even Tamara's entry into a convent does not save her: she finally surrenders, but dies with the Demon's first kiss:

> The deadly poison of his kiss
> Instantly penetrated her breast.
> A tormented, terrible cry
> Broke into the silence of the night.
> In it there was everything: love, suffering,
> A reproach with a final prayer
> And a hopeless farewell—
> Farewell to young life.

When Tamara is buried in the family chapel on a lofty peak, the Demon claims her soul, but an angel descends from the heavens, rejects the Demon's claim, and bears her aloft. Once more the Demon is condemned to his eternal fate:

> And again he remained, haughty,
> Alone, as before, in the universe
> Without hope or love!

The above is a straightforward plot synopsis of the final reworking of *The Demon*. It exists in eight recognized versions,
however. Lermontov began *The Demon* in 1829, when he was only
fourteen, and continued to revise and expand upon his original
idea for nearly a decade. The first five versions are the so-called
early, pre-Caucasus ones, in which the action is set vaguely during
the Spanish Inquisition, the heroine is a nun, and the narration
is both abstract and autobiographical. These early versions date
respectively from 1829 (I), early 1830 (II), 1831 (III and IV),
and 1832–33 (V). Version III bears an epigraph from Byron's
Cain, which clearly had a decisive influence on Lermontov's concept; and a dedication to "Madonna," i.e., to Varenka Lopukhina,
with whom the work continued to be associated in Lermontov's
mind. He imagined her as the heroine and himself (at sixteen)
as the Demon: "Like a demon, cold and stern / I took pleasure
in doing evil in the world. . . ."

Lermontov's first exile to the Caucasus provided several ideas
for his poem. He changed the setting to the Caucasus and made
the time more contemporary. Both these changes were salutary.
The setting of the early versions had been nebulous and not very
believable. In the Caucasus, however, Lermontov felt at home.
He rarely describes nature in the North, but in the South his
imagination is fired by its majestic peaks, deep gorges, and rushing streams, as well as its proud and beautiful inhabitants. His
descriptions of this magnificent scenery energize the poem.

Setting the poem in a more contemporary time also eliminated
a problem. Lermontov had no feeling for history; he was interested
in the display of feelings. A contemporaneous time for his poem
allowed him to avoid problems of specific historical context
gracefully.

He introduced these changes in 1838, adding a new dedication
to the Caucasus. He produced a sketch (the Erevan manuscript)
which, with a few minor additions and variations, became version

VI. This is the so-called "Lopukhin Version," the only one of the three mature versions to survive in an authorized copy. Dated 8 September 1838 and sent as a gift to Varenka, it is the first version to include the justly famous song beginning "On an ethereal ocean." It also contains for the first time the Dedication, placed at the end of the poem, which opens:

> I have finished—and feel in my breast an involuntary doubt!
> Will the long familiar note engage you once again,
> The pensive singing of unfamiliar lines,
> You, forgetful yet unforgotten friend?

There are unusually lovely assonances in the original Russian:

> Ya konchil—i v grudi nevolnoe somnenie
> Zaymyot li vnov tebya davno znakomyzvuk,
> Stikhov nevedomykh zadumchivoe penie,
> Tebya, zabyvchivy, no nezabvennydrug?

The Caucasus, then, had provided Lermontov with solutions to problems of setting and time inherent in the early drafts. Lermontov continued to revise version VI, but for prosaic, not poetical, reasons, and now made a serious attempt to have the poem published.[3] In version VI the heroine is named for the first time. She is not a nun originally, but only enters the convent after the death of her bridegroom in order to escape the temptations of the Demon. Hereafter the poem is divided into two parts, with the second part taking place in the convent.

Lermontov now makes a major change in Tamara's fate, obviously for the purpose of getting the poem past the censors. He "saves" Tamara: her soul, beginning with version VII, ascends to heaven. We know version VII was completed and dated 4 December 1838, but it has not survived. Unlike version VI, it did not circulate widely in manuscript.

In early 1839 Lermontov returned to *The Demon* for the last time. The Empress Alexandra Fyodorovna expressed an interest in reading it, and Lermontov prepared a manuscript for her, version VIII. The Empress noted in her diary that she read it on 9 February. On 10 February the manuscript was returned to Lermontov with word that Her Majesty had deigned to like the work. Encouraged by this piece of good fortune, Lermontov submitted it to the censors a month later. For a while things seemed to go well, but in the end all his changes were to no avail. The poem's religious theme made the poem suspect not only to state censorship, but even more to church censorship. At this point apparently Lermontov himself accepted the situation and decided, quite wisely, that there was no point in trying to publish such a controversial work.

In *The Demon* Lermontov grappled with a theme that had been treated by many Romantic poets since the discovery, or rather reinterpretation, of Milton's *Paradise Lost*. The Christian Satan and the pagan Prometheus were the two seminal mythic figures of the Romantic period, symbolizing rejection of a cruel world created by an unjust god. The direct and indirect sources of Lermontov's poem are so numerous that there is little point in identifying them one by one. Duchesne argues for the precedence of personal characteristics over literary borrowings in the figure of the Demon:

Thus the poet mixed together in this figure of the Demon traits which literary tradition furnished him and those which a patient analysis had revealed to him deep in his own soul: the latter play a much more important part. This explains the insignificance of the character of Tamara.[4]

The last sentence points up the basic fact that once again a long and ambitious work of Lermontov's consists for the most part of a monologue by the hero. Other characters—more specifically, the heroine—receive little attention.

Moreover, even if we discount the modern temperament's distaste for Romantic posturing, Lermontov has not really done justice to his theme. Lermontov suffers from the fact that his demonic theme was later treated with consummate artistry by Dostoevsky. To read Lermontov's works now is to feel that an important and complex topic is being handled in an intellectually impoverished context. Dostoevsky's demons are much more persuasive than Lermontov's because they are endowed with more powerful rhetorical skill. Dostoevsky's demonic figures must defend their positions, while Lermontov's do not because he is too obviously in sympathy with them.

To be sure, Soviet Russian scholars have written a great deal about the "philosophical" content of *The Demon*. For me that is too grand a term. Lermontov's Demon is a passionate disciple of Milton's Satan and Byron's Cain; he is not interested in ideas or questions of theodicy in the same way that Dostoevsky's Ivan Karamazov is a generation later.

Lermontov's Demon behaves remarkably like a Hussar officer. He is chasing after a woman, while at the same time he longs for the serene pleasures of Paradise, when he knew "neither malice, nor doubt" (1:1). He is not as consistently defiant as Satan or Lucifer. He has even become bored with doing evil: "Ruling the worthless earth / He sowed evil without pleasure" (1:2) In fact, the Demon has reached a stage of cosmic boredom. He despises or hates everything and everybody; the gorgeous scenery of the Caucasus arouses only "cold" envy within him.

Sometimes the descriptions of the Demon descend to banality as Lermontov tries to maintain a melodramatic tone:

> . . . but the proud spirit
> Cast a supercilious eye over his God's creation,
> And on his lofty forehead nothing was reflected. (1:3.)

But if the reader accepts this extravagant claim, he is disillusioned when the Demon first sees Tamara, in section 5, as she descends to the Aragva River for water. Tamara's father is Prince Gudal, whose castle high on a rock is bustling with preparations for her wedding to the Prince of the mythical kingdom of Sinodal. Tamara dances and sings with her handmaidens, and the narrator swears that no more beautiful girl ever lived. He also seems to regret that she, "playful child of freedom," must marry and therefore become a "sad slave." But when the Demon sees Tamara:

> The desert of his mute soul
> Was filled with heavenly music,
> And again he perceived the blessings
> Of love, goodness and beauty! (1:9)

The strongly held beliefs of the "proud spirit" vanish instantaneously. Such lightning changes of mood, insufficiently motivated, belong to melodrama rather than to tragedy.

This passage linking the vision of a beautiful Georgian maiden with "heavenly music" recalls a similar episode in *The Novice.* The novice catches sight of the maiden descending to fill her jug with water as she sings a song. The song intensifies the novice's enjoyment of his surroundings, and his sense of freedom. It serves also as a prelude to the happiness he believes he will find when he returns home. But the notion of "home," as we have seen, is associated with an ideal existence to which the novice strains to escape. In *The Demon,* on the other hand, we have, as it were, a literal desire on the hero's part to escape to Paradise.

Now the Demon recalls earlier times, presumably in heaven, when he could feel both joy and sorrow. (The music awakened in his soul is also literally "heavenly," since the Demon once heard such music in heaven.) He can no longer forget those times, and he does not wish to: "Forget?—God would not grant forgetfulness: / And in any case he would not have accepted it" (1:9). Curiously enough, however, the Demon's immediate reaction to such blissful feelings is to arrange for the murder of Tamara's bridegoom, again without sufficient motivation. The reader is puzzled by the abrupt alternation of the Demon's new, good feelings with his evil action. Lermontov misses the opportunity for an agonizing soliloquy by his hero. This is very surprising in a writer who has now gained, through *A Hero of Our Time,* a reputation for psychological insight. Perhaps Lermontov simply felt bound by the style and generic expectations of the Byronic narrative poem. Only in prose fiction could he fully explore the contradictory motivations of his characters.

At the beginning of Part II Tamara has decided to enter a convent in order to enlist God's assistance in escaping the Demon's advances. Despite her father's disappointment, Tamara refuses to consider any other suitors, explaining that the Demon, the spirit of cunning, torments her with "an irresistible dream."

The remainder of Part II describes Tamara's unavailing efforts to resist the Demon's overtures. Unlike the novice and many other Lermontovian figures, she has entered the cloister *willingly*, to flee from temptation. The denouement is delayed by lush descriptions of the convent, the Caucasus's luxuriant valleys and snow-capped mountains, and Tamara's turbulent emotions. Before long Tamara, despite herself, yearns to see the Demon: "She might want to pray to the saints—/ But her heart prayed to *him*." (2:6). The Demon, too, finds himself moved; he feels love, and even more the "anguish of love," for the first time. He enters the convent determined to love selflessly and to start a new life. But in Tamara's cell he finds an angel sent to defend her honor. Challenged by the angel, the Demon undergoes an alarming change of heart:

> And again in his soul there awoke
> The poison of ancient hatred.
> "She is mine!" he said threateningly,
> "Leave her alone, she is mine!" (2:9)

The phrase "And again" (*I vnov*) is one Lermontov uses a great deal in describing sudden changes in the emotions or attitude of his characters. It is a weak device, and reminds one of similar key words like "suddenly" favored by Leo Tolstoy, another writer who had difficulty in depicting his characters gaining awareness or reaching a new plateau of cognition. The frequent use of the phrase "and again" may be linked with Lermontov's belief that happiness is fleeting, that sooner rather than later life will return to its familiar routine. Life is cyclical, but the evil cycles are more tenacious than the good.

When Tamara declares that she can never love him, the Demon embarks on a confession of the type that Lermontov's rejected heroes usually deliver. To be sure, the verse is technically on a high level and the speech is a splendid piece of rhetoric. The reader, however, is likely to sympathize with Tamara's brisk reply: "What need have I to know of your sorrows, / Why do you complain to me?" (2:10). But a moment later she has weakened, asking the demon to swear he really will change his wicked ways as he has promised. The Demon is happy to swear by everything imaginable for the next twenty lines. Then he paints a splendid picture of their life together, promising that she will reign over the earth, and that he will give her jewels and gifts beyond number. Tamara says nothing, but she must surely be impressed.

As the Demon bends over to kiss her, poison pours from his burning lips into her heart, and she dies with but a single cry. As Tamara's soul is carried up to heaven by an angel, the Demon confronts them and demands Tamara's return to him. Tamara is frightened, for he is now revealed to her as the spirit of darkness. This time the angel defends her, telling the Demon that God in His wisdom has spared her soul because she has endured enough pain and sorrow already:

> She has suffered and loved—
> And paradise is open to love.

The Demon is left to curse his fate and his foolish dreams.

The Demon became one of Lermontov's best-known works. It was particularly popular around the turn of the century, when the Symbolist period witnessed a great revival of interest in Romanticism. Indeed, Russian Symbolism, like French Symbolism, to which it owes so much, could be viewed as a kind of neo-Romanticism. Still, Lermontov's poem had more impact on the other arts than it did on poetry. We have noted that Anton Rubinstein wrote an opera based on *The Demon,* and it enjoyed some popularity then. The important Russian painter Mikhail Vrubel, who went mad in 1905 and died five years later, was fascinated by the image of the Demon and executed a series of paintings based on Lermontov's work, in a fruitless search for an absolute, total freedom of expression.

Lermontov's good friend and admirer, Shan-Girey, did not care for *The Demon.* He compared it to an opera in which the music was charming, but the libretto absolute rubbish (*Vosp.*, 45). This is not an unfair comment, for the librettos of many famous operas,

*"The Demon Seated", painted in oils by
Vrubel (1890).*

if read without music, seem rather silly. This holds also if one
reads *The Demon* without hearing the music of its poetry in the
original Russian.

Even the poetry, the chief glory of the poem, sometimes seems
melodic filigree. After all, the work consists for the most part
of a very long monologue. There is no plot to speak of. Presumably
the Demon can have Tamara whenever he wishes since she is a
mere mortal without heavenly support until she dies. Why does
the angel refuse to help at first, or why is he unable to help?

Because God has not reached a decision in her case? These un-
answered questions remain unanswerable. Lermontov provides no
philosophical keys to the poem, since it basically lacks philosophy. It contains some of the most beautiful lines in the history
of Russian verse, but significantly it had no poetic imitators.
When it was finally first published in Russia in 1860, it must
have seemed like a museum piece. But the Demon, transmogrified
into Pechorin, the central character of *A Hero of Our Time,* did
have an enormous impact on Russian literature.

Sashka

As early as 1831, at the outset of his career when *The Demon*
was still in embryo, Lermontov reminded himself in a note to
"write a long satirical poem on the adventures of the Demon"
(4:344). This is the first indication of Lermontov's interest in the
comic or ironical side of Byron's legacy. But apart from a few
sketches of 1831–32, he began writing "long satirical poems"
only when he moved to St. Petersburg.

In his unfinished poem *Sashka* (the hero's name), written in
1834–36, Lermontov attempted to move from the vulgar farce
of his "Hussar poems" to the higher level of irony. As usual, he
borrowed lines and stanzas from earlier works, but essentially
Sashka was a new departure. Furthermore, all through it we find
tongue-in-cheek references to Lermontov's seriously intended
Romantic poems. Such parody indicates his growing maturity
and self-awareness, though he did not abandon his earlier style
and themes even in the late 1830s, well after *Sashka* was written.

Though subtitled "A Moral Poem," it soon becomes clear that
Sashka is no such thing. Rather it describes a wealthy, young,
aristocratic man-about-town, who spends his time partying,
drinking, and chasing women. The whole concept of the poem,
including its frequent digressions and its bantering tone, has
much in common with Pushkin's *Eugene Onegin,* except that the
setting is Moscow, not St. Petersburg. Just as Pushkin's narrator
recalls his friendship with Onegin, Lermontov's narrator declares
he was a friend of his hero, who had recently died abroad.

Following the example of *Eugene Onegin,* Lermontov devotes
several opening stanzas to the conceit that he (or the narrator)

and his Muse are traveling across Moscow together in the snow
seeking the house to which Sashka will himself soon come:

> Let us walk through the snow, my muse, only be quiet
> And raise your skirt as high as you can. (stanza 11)

The poem now enters upon (for fully a third of its length) a
description of the hero and an account of his visit to this house,
which we discover is a bawdy house. There Sashka finds two
young women. He spends a rapturous hour with one of them,
but the details are passed over in coy silence by the usually
loquacious narrator. As the couple lie in bed, the beautiful young
harlot, Tirza—daughter of a Polish Jew—persuades Sashka to
take her, incognito, to the theater or a ball dressed up as a high-
society lady.

At this point the narrator declares that, since his hero is asleep,
he cannot go forward with the plot and will instead recount the
story of Sashka's origins, childhood, and youth.

After some time, in stanza 121, the narrator finally returns
to the scene at the whorehouse. It is now supposedly the "morning
after." Sashka awakes, dresses, and departs, thinking happily
about the fun he will have tricking snobbish society by introducing Tirza as a young lady of fashion, for she has two great
disabilities in the eyes of Russian society: she is a prostitute and
she is Jewish. The poem then ends with the mocking assurance:
"There's an end to everything—/ Napoleons, storms, and wars."

The narrative voice in *Sashka* is playful, coy, bantering, and
sometimes even serious. The serious tone intrudes, however, only
when the narrator discusses his own feelings, not Sashka's. Quite
often Lermontov undercuts apparently serious lines in a manner
that comes close to parody of his own earlier Byronic works. For
example, in describing his hero, the narrator says:

> Oh, if he could, clad in lightning,
> With one blow, destroy the whole world!
> (But happily for you, dear reader,
> He was not endowed with such power.) (73)

In the following stanza the narrator mocks the contemporary
fashion for psychological analysis:

> I will not undertake, like a psychologist,
> To turn Sashka's character inside out
> And display it like a pie with truffles. (74)

Lermontov even makes fun of his own pain at the sudden and—
as he viewed it—treacherous marriage of Varenka Lopukhina in
1835. After describing Tirza, the narrator turns to the other girl,
plump but attractive, whose name is Varyusha (a nickname for
Varvara): "And so, to avoid evil, we will / Rechristen our Varyusha and call her Parasha" (24).

Lermontov's inconsistency in narrative point of view and his
failure to maintain or even establish an acceptable relationship
with both his hero and his reader are the great weaknesses of the
poem. I speak here not of the way Lermontov undercuts his
melodramatic statements or his emotional hyperbole, but rather
of his failure to distinguish his narrator from his hero, of his
failure to "escape the self." Lermontov indulges in the same *étalage
du moi* as in the earlier poems, where the narrator is an overwhelming presence. Even the hero fades into the background.
When the narrator describes Sashka's feelings as a lonely, abused
child, his tone is artificial and awkward; we feel we are learning
more about the narrator then the hero.

The digressions on the narrator's own feelings and history assume a life of their own, and are often not connected at all with
the plot. For instance, a stanza making fun of panegyric odes
leads to a personal aside in which the narrator announces how
and where he wishes to be buried. Then he changes his mind
and decides he wants no trace of himself to remain: let his ashes
be scattered to the wind, let his soul fuse with that of the universe.
He declares that in this life he has drunk poison drop by drop,
but nobody paid any attention:

And from that time my tongue tasted
The same poison, and in search of a just revenge
I began to denigrate the crowd under the cover of flattery. . . . (84)

Apparently conscious that he has overstepped the mark, Lermontov abruptly returns to his hero. Unfortunately, this moment of lucidity passes all too soon, and before long the narrator is regaling us once again with witty asides and personal reflections.

The poem simply breaks off after 149 stanzas. We never learn whether Tirza passes successfully as a high-society lady. It is true, the fragment was a recognized subgenre during the Romantic period, but at 149 stanzas *Sashka* is rather long for a fragment. In any case, Lermontov adumbrates a plot of sorts, and it is logical to assume that he meant to pursue the work. But he did not do so.

The Tambov Treasurer's Wife

It may be less than fair to criticize *Sashka,* a work Lermontov did not regard as finished and made no attempt to publish. We discover similar problems of structure, characterization, and narrative stance in another poem which he did publish in 1838: *Tambovskaya kaznacheysha* [The Tambov Treasurer's Wife].

The poem is an attempt to sanitize for public consumption the sort of amorous adventures he had described during his Hussar period. It is set in the Russian provinces, and the shenanigans it describes recall those in Pushkin's *Count Nulin.* Lermontov also uses the Onegin stanza, though he notes he will be accused of being old fashioned.

The poem consists of 53 stanzas, about the number in one canto of *Onegin.* The verse is of high caliber. Undoubtedly, Lermontov was deliberately matching his skills against Pushkin's and comes off well in the comparison, which is high praise indeed. In areas beyond technique and versification, however, Lermontov's poem falters.

The opening six stanzas, in the best tradition of Pushkin and Gogol, mockingly praise the charming elegance of what is clearly a typically grubby Russian provincial town. The arrival of a new regiment of lancers to garrison the town causes great excitement, just as in a host of other Russian works, for example, Gogol's splendid short story "Kolyaska" [The Carriage] of 1836, or Chekhov's play *Tri sestry* [Three Sisters] of 1901.

The example of both Pushkin and Gogol is visible also in Lermontov's careful selection of detail, the many fine touches in the opening stanzas. The original Russian has a snap that is lost in translation, as when Lermontov contrasts delicate young ladies at their windows to the tired, dust-blown cavalry riding into town:

> I lyubopytno probegayut
> Glaza opukhshie devits
> Ryady surovykh, pylnykh lits. (5)

the English translation cannot hope to match the original:

> And curious glances are cast
> By the sleepy eyes of maidens
> Upon the rows of stern, dusty faces.

Lermontov utilizes Pushkin's own technique of rounding off a stanza powerfully when he describes the lancers' rearguard:

> Tolpa malchishek gorodskikh
> Nemytykh, shumnykh i bosykh. (6)

The translation of this last rhyming couplet demonstrates the tonal alteration after the preceding lines:

> A mob of lads from the town,
> Unwashed, noisy, and barefoot.

All the government officials in Tambov are as corrupt as those in any "town of N" described by Gogol. For instance, Tambov's treasurer Bobkovsky is a thorough rascal. He is old and bald-headed, and naturally married to a much younger woman, Avdotya Nikolaevna (or Dunya). His chief passion, however, is gambling at cards. Stealing from the treasury and cheating at the gaming table leave him little time for the attractive and lonely Dunya, who could potentially be a fascinating character if only she received more attention from the narrator than from her husband, In the event, though he catalogues her charms at great length, she remains a shadowy figure.

Eykhenbaum has noted that in his dedication the narrator refers to the work as a *skazka* ("tale" or "fairy tale"). But he fails to observe that the narrator also calls it a *roman* ("novel" or "romance," stanza 13) and a *rasskaz* ("story," stanza 45). The point is that all three generic terms characterize types of prose fiction, rather than types of verse. The confusion is not Lermontov's alone, but is a part of the general trend toward prose fiction during the 1830s in Russia.

Lermontov sets the scene for the hero, Captain Garin, to besiege Avdotya Nikolaevna's virtue by billeting the officers in the Hotel Moscow, which stands opposite the Bobkovsky mansion. Once again, the narrator declares himself a friend of the hero and insists that the events he will describe actually took place five years ago.

After this effort to gain the reader's confidence, the narrator gives a lengthy account of Garin's life and habits, interrupted by occasional asides and witticisms. Lermontov's reader does not know whether to admire or despise Garin. Garin is a roughneck, who gets by with a combination of luck, the help of friends, and a large measure of ruthlessness. We learn, for example, the "As a joke once after a quarrel, / He put a bullet between the eyes of a friend" (16). In the end we lack the inside view of Garin that might provide some understanding of the man.

Dunya is an obvious target for a man like Garin. She is young and neglected, and her own sister describes the satisfactions of a liaison with a cavalry officer. The narrator passes coyly over this account of the charm of cavalry moustaches, but Dunya is curious.

Lermontov now sets the scene for a staple of farce. Garin invades the mansion and importunes Dunya on his knees. Naturally Bobkovsky discovers them, and Garin departs hurriedly, to prepare for the challenge to a duel that he knows must inevitably follow.

Much to his surprise, however, Bobkovsky sends him an invitation to a whist party instead of a challenge, for unclear reasons. The reader might expect that since Bobkovsky is as experienced at cards as Garin is in seducing neglected wives, he plans to fleece and humiliate the officer rather than meet him on the dueling ground, where a military man would naturally have the advantage. But in fact neither man succeeds at his own forte.

Garin arrives at the whist party, to be treated politely by Bobkovsky, as though nothing had happened. When guests and host sit down to cards, Bobkovsky soon loses everything he possesses, an outcome which strains our credulity since we had earlier been told of Bobkovsky's gambling prowess. Even more astonishingly, Bobkovsky stakes his wife on a last bid to recover his fortune. Garin accepts the challenge, and wins.

Suddenly the emotional tone changes as the narrator turns his attention to Dunya:

> What she felt then—
> I will not try to explain to you;
> Her face expressed
> So many torments that perhaps,
> Had you been able to read her expression,
> You could not have helped crying. (50)

But she says nothing; she rises from her chair and walks to the gambling table where her husband is sitting:

> She looked at her husband
> And hurled into his face
> Her wedding ring— (51)
>
> And swooned . . . (52)

The triumphant Garin gathers her up in his arms and strides out of the house. The stanzaic enjambement and the omission of the verb in the Russian original make the scene more intensely vivid:

> Ona na muzha posmotrela
> I brosila emu v litso
> Svoyo venchalnoe koltso—(51)
>
> I v obmorok . . . (52)

This is high melodrama—and yet there is something wrong.

The problem, I would suggest, is that in assembling his material Lermontov has not combined its various elements into a consistent whole. At the end the tone changes from bantering to serious. A tale of "flat," farcical characters, with whom the reader need not sympathize, suddenly becomes a melodrama, which demands our sympathies for its participants. In terms of Pushkin's works, it is a switch from *Count Nulin* to one of the Belkin tales, "The Shot." To be sure, in Pushkin's *Onegin* the mood changes, but that is a much longer work, and the colors darken gradually over both fictional time and the time it takes to read it. But Lermontov does not establish the right tone for his work and fails to define an appropriate narrative stance. These general questions of narrative stance, along with the escape from the "I," are the two obstacles Lermontov had to overcome to mature as a writer.

Song of the Merchant Kalashnikov

I now turn to two late narrative poems which demonstrate Lermontov's growing mastery of the problems of narrative stance and the Byronic hero whose solution had eluded him previously.

One poem—*Pesnya pro tsarya Ivana Vasilievicha, molodogo oprichnika i udalogo kuptsa Kalashnikova* [Song of the Tsar Ivan Vasilievich, the young oprichnik and the Bold Merchant Kalashnikov]— was completed and published in Lermontov's lifetime. The other, *Skazka dlya detey* [A Fairytale for Children], remained unfinished and did not appear in print until a year after his death. In character and tone the two works are quite different. The first is a stylized folk tale set during the reign of Ivan the Terrible, while the second is an elegant and ironical work on St. Petersburg high society.

Nothing illustrates more clearly the compressed nature of Lermontov's development and the wide variety of styles with which he experimented simultaneously than the fact that his *Song of the Merchant Kalashnikov* was published in 1838, the same year as *The Tambov Treasurer's Wife. Kalashnikov* is unique among Lermontov's narrative poems in its classical simplicity, Homeric objectivity, and selection of detail. The reader of Russian derives great pleasure from the poem's rhythmical lines, reminiscent of folk meters.

Kalashnikov stands out among Lermontov's narrative poems for its consistent narrative viewpoint. It is not a monologue by a hero complaining about his fate. The distinction between hero and narrator is not blurred. In fact, the narrator is a stylized "singer" in the old Russian folk tradition who does not address the "reader" at all: his audience are his fellow singers and the boyar Matvey Romodanovsky and his lady. This could not be used as a general solution to the questions of narrative technique, especially in prose fiction, but for *Kalashnikov* it is totally successful.

In the best epic tradition, the singer plunges directly into the story, *in medias res.* At the court of Ivan the Terrible the Tsar notes that one of his favorite guards (*oprichniki*) is downcast. Asked the reason by the Tsar, the *oprichnik* Kiribeevich responds that he has fallen in love with a beautiful girl from a merchant family, Alyona Dmitrievna, but she will have nothing to do with him. The Tsar, sympathetic, gives him jewelry and other gifts, advising him to get a matchmaker and seek the girl's hand in marriage, but not to worry if he is rejected: "If you win her love, then celebrate your wedding. / If not, then don't be angry!" The original Russian of these two lines with the dactylic endings is typical of the lilting rhythm pervading the entire poem:

> Kak polyúbishsya—prázdnuy svádebku,
> Ne polyúbishsya—ne progneváysya!

At this point the singer intrudes to say that Kiribeevich has misled the Tsar by omitting the pertinent fact that Alyona Dmitrievna is already married, and to the real hero of the tale, Stepan Paramonovich Kalashnikov, a successful and hard-working merchant in the silk trade.

He is introduced in Part II, as the scene shifts to the Kalshnikov home. Kalashnikov waits impatiently for this wife to return from church; when she does, she is in tears, and her clothes are torn. At first Kalsahnikov is angry, but his wife explains that Kiribeevich accosted her on her way back from church. He had refused to let her pass, offered her gifts, laid hands upon her, and kissed her.

The singer passes over Kalashnikov's reaction, sparing us the gnashing of teeth, tearing of hair, and swearing of vengeance. Instead Kalashnikov summons his two younger brothers to tell them what has happened, but very briefly. Then, in a matter-of-fact manner, he declares he will fight Kiribeevich the next day in the boxing matches scheduled to be held on the ice of the Moscow River in the presence of the Tsar. Kalshnikov will try to kill the man who has dishonored his wife, but if he is killed then his brothers are to challenge Kiribeevich themselves one after the other and fight to the death for the family honor. The brothers accept this as their duty unquestioningly.

The singer sets the scene on the following day with an elaborate description of Moscow and a personification of the dawn. Here Lermontov's lyricism is quite appropriate, neither random nor capricious. It is called forth by the specific needs of the story line, as the singer frames the action with a description of beautiful, indifferent nature. Lermontov avoids the Romantic "pathetic fallacy."

The boxing match between Kalashnikov and the *oprichnik* is narrated with remarkable economy, not only for Lermontov but also for the Russian folklore tradition, in which such crucial battles are commonly narrated in epic detail and at great length. The actual combat between the two men is equally brief. Kiribeevich strikes first, hitting Kalashnikov in the chest. The bold merchant, gathering all his strength, retaliates with a mighty blow to the side of the head. Kiribeevich is killed instantly.

The Tsar is angered at the unexpected death of his *oprichnik,* a famous fighter, and he demands to know why Kalashnikov has killed Kiribeevich. The merchant respectfully replies that he will only explain to God, but he admits freely that he killed his opponent deliberately. Neither the singer nor Kalashnikov protests when the Tsar sentences him to death. Indeed, the Tsar displays his mercy by promising to take care of Kalashnikov's family and to have the ax sharpened so as to give him a quick and easy death.

Lermontov's most un-Byronic and undemonic hero is grateful to the Tsar, and the two men part with mutual respect. Theirs is a society in which certain things are done and others are not; in which authority is accepted; in which honor and duty govern one's behavior, not the "rights" of the individual or the passions. Elsewhere, as we have seen, Lermontov manipulated his material, from whatever source, in typically Romantic fashion. Here he has accepted the atmosphere of the genre he is imitiating, acknowledging its artistic integrity. For once, we need not filter a work of Lermontov's through his personality.

By no means does the singer praise the *oprichnik* or the Tsar. A few brief, oblique comments by Kalashnikov and his wife indicate that the *oprichnik* is notorious for his behavior. The singer's audience is meant to suffer with the brave merchant. His fate is called "cruel and shameful," and yet everything is seen in epic perspective. The singer ends the third and final section of his story just as he has the previous two—with a cheerful refrain addressed to his fellow *gusla* players urging them to do honor to their audience—the boyar and his fair lady, as well as to all Christian folk in the land.

In his youth Lermontov regretted not having had a Russian nurse who might have introduced him to Russian folk tales, which he felt were worth all of French literature. *Kalashnikov* shows Lermontov must have made good the omission in the intervening years, because the poem gives clear evidence of his close familiarity with Russian folklore. We do not know how he came by this knowledge. We do know that national folklore material was eagerly collected and imitated during the Romantic period, and not only in Russia. Poets and historians saw folklore as a means of establishing cultural roots apart from both the ancient Classical heritage and also French literature, which had dominated European letters since the seventeenth century.

Kalashnikov captures both the tone of the *byliny* and their characteristic singing rhythm. It is written in lines of eleven or twelve syllables carrying three or four strong stresses per line, but there is no regular alternation of stressed and unstressed syllables. The lines are not rhymed, but do end in dactyls. Thus the poem's lines contrast strongly with the iambs and trochees and rhymed lines that had already become the standard for Russian poetry at the time Lermontov was writing.

The following lines will illustrate the rhythm and tone of the poem, together with its stylized folk epithets and formulae, which in fact Lermontov uses more frequently than is the rule in Russian folk tales:

> I uslyshav to, Alyona Dmitrevna
> Zadrozhav vsya, moya golubushka,
> Zatryaslas, kak listochek osinovy,
> Gorko-gorko ona vosplakalas,
> V nogi muzhu povalilasya.
> "Gosudár ty moy, krasno solnyshko,
> Il ubey menya ili vyslushay!
> Tvoi rechi—budto ostrynozh;
> Ot nikh serdtse razryvaetsya.
> Ne boyusya smerti lyutyya,
> Ne boyusya ya lyudskoy molvy,
> A' boyus tvoey nemilosti."

The following literal translation cannot match the rhythm of the original or render the connotations of the words and phrases taken from the Russian folklore tradition:

> And having heard this, Alyona Dmitrevna,
> Trembling all over, my poor dear,
> Began to shake like an aspen leaf,
> Bitter, bitter tears she shed,
> And threw herself at her husband's feet.
> "My lord, my beautiful sun,
> Either kill me or hear me out!
> Your words are like a sharp knife;
> My heart is breaking because of them.
> I do not fear cruel death,
> I do not fear people's gossip,
> But I fear your displeasure."

Kalashnikov is a remarkably successful stylization of the so-called "historical songs," a folk genre popular since the time of Ivan the Terrible. Lermontov has taken some liberties with his material, fusing, as he does, different *bylina* (heroic epic) traditions and cycles of historical songs. It is not clear whether Lermontov realized he was mingling disparate elements, but in any case high literature has always manipulated popular literature for its own purposes.

Kalashnikov melds two basic folk cycles.[5] The first opens with the Tsar at a feast surrounded by his courtiers. One is sad; responding to the tsar's questions, he says he has fallen in love. The Tsar gives him gifts and wishes him good fortune. The remainder of such tales typically describes the man's quest for the beloved. Within the tradition, though, the *oprichnik* Kiribeevich should be the hero instead of the villain.

The entry of Kalashnikov and his wife introduces the second type of tale in which the husband seeks revenge for the dishonoring of his wife. Often the outraged husband kills his wife; in other variants the husband returns home to find his wife faithful but forced into a wedding with another man. (cf. *The Odyssey*).

Lermontov also departs from tradition in his portrayal of the relationship between the Tsar and Kalashnikov. The hero should be torn between his sense of duty to the Tsar and his desire for revenge. The Tsar should be angry with him not because he has killed the *oprichnik,* but because he declines the Tsar's offer of gifts and an invitation to enter his service.

All too often Soviet comment on *Kalashnikov* focuses on the "tyrannical" Tsar, attempting to portray Kalashnikov as a sort of proto-Decembrist radical. In fact, however, the Tsar is not shown as a tyrant, and even if he were he plays a minor role in the poem. Furthermore, far from being rebellious, Kalashnikov is a devoted subject of the Tsar. Equally misguided are attempts to decipher the poem as a disguised account of Pushkin's death in a duel over his wife's honor. Such politicized interpretations are an unfortunate legacy of Socialist Realism.

To be sure, Lermontov introduces some of his favorite ideas and themes in this poem, albeit in an uncharacteristically reticent manner. Kalashnikov is undemonic, but he is proud, independent, and something of a merchant "outsider" in Muscovite society.

Furthermore, he seeks and achieves revenge, which is one of Lermontov's most enduring themes.

Further, in a manner much less obtrusive than in other works, but nevertheless apparent and quite in tune with the Romantic view of history, Lermontov presents his hero as a man far superior to his, Lermontov's, own contemporaries.

For once, Lermontov does not dot all the "i's" and cross all the "t's." He allows his reader to draw some conclusions himself. Very often Lermontov lacks faith in his audience, and sometimes has no clear image of who his audience is, except in love lyrics and epistles. *Kalashnikov* is a notable exception, possibly because the poet has depicted the audience within the poem itself.

A Fairy Tale for Children

Lermontov's last attempt at a narrative poem, or a tale in verse, promised to be one of his most successful works, but he did not live to complete it. He wrote *A Fairy Tale for Children* in 1840, just one year after he had completed the final version of *The Demon* and a short while after he had put the finishing touches to *A Hero of Our Time*. Both *A Fairy Tale* and the novel may be regarded as attempts on Lermontov's part to re-explore the demonic theme and the Byronic hero from a more mature perspective. Though I am discussing *Kalashnikov* and *A Fairy Tale for Children* together, they are diametrically opposed in subject matter, tone, and setting. *Kalashnikov* was completed and published during the poet's lifetime, whereas *A Fairy Tale* appeared in 1842, after the poet's death. Even the title was devised by an editor, who drew upon an ironical statement in the second stanza that the work is a "fairy tale" (*skazka*) with a moral at the end, which will therefore be suitable for children.

The artistic progress Lermontov has made in a very short time becomes evident if we compare this poem with *Sashka*. Superficially, the poems are similar. The twenty-seven completed stanzas of *A Fairy Tale* have exactly the same meter (iambic pentameter) and the same rhyme scheme (AbAbAccDDee) as *Sashka*. Gone, however, are the long-winded, random, lyrical digressions as well as the "witty" asides. Now the narrator does not seek to dominate both characters and story line. Furthermore, the tone is more balanced, without the extremes of cynicism and melodrama that are such a prominent feature of *Sashka*. Even unfinished as it stands, *A Fairy Tale* marks the culmination of Lermontov's efforts to produce a light, ironical narrative poem in the manner of *Don Juan* or *Eugene Onegin*.

But there is an implicit difficulty in this comparison. By 1840 the age of the witty, ironical poem was over. Lermontov begins *A Fairy Tale* with the lines:

> The age of epic poems has long since passed,
> And tales in verse have fallen into decline;
> Poets are not entirely at fault in this
> (Although many lack a really smooth line);
> And the public has something to answer for, too.

The narrator declares that he himself no longer reads verse (everyone nowadays is too busy), but he still enjoys scribbling poetry. Then he introduces his hero, a type he admits to having portrayed before:

> Burning with the flame and power of youthful years,
> I used to sing of a different demon:
> That was a mad, passionate, childish raving.

The poet wonders whether some young woman might be reading this earlier work now or whether it provides dusty food for mice, in an obvious reference to version VI of *The Demon*, which he had given in 1838 to Varvara Lopukhina.

Clearly Lermontov has found this image of the demon difficult to escape. In stanza 6 he writes:

> My youthful mind used to be disturbed
> By a powerful image; among other visions,
> Like a tsar, mute and proud, it shone
> With such a magical sweet beauty,
> That I was frightened . . . and my soul by ennui
> Was gripped—and this wild delirium
> Pursued my reason for many years.

> But I, bidding farewell to similar dreams,
> Rid myself of it also—in verse!

Thus Lermontov himself recognizes how powerful this image had been in his work, and for himself personally. These lines also show how far he has come from the scabrous verse of his Hussar period. Now he can step back and view the image of the Demon calmly but critically.

In stanza 4 the poet invites us into a sumptuous bedroom where a girl is sleeping. In the last lines of the stanza, the reader suddenly realizes that he is not alone:

> Against the muslin of the lace pillows
> Is silhouetted a young, but severe profile . . .
> And at it gazes Mephistopheles.

Lermontov must have been pleased with the startling rhyme *prófil / Mefistófel*. The use of the name Mephistopheles points to the transformation of the melodramatic, gloomy Demon into a totally new type, obviously borrowed from Goethe's *Faust:* witty, self-assured, sophisticated.

Lermontov's new devil resembles the old Demon in his passion for beauty and his tendency to fall in love, but he does not rant and rage or protest his fate. His love for the sleeping Nina appears quite genuine; but it is a pleasure, not a torment. There is no indication that Nina offers him an escape, or indeed that he is searching for salvation.

The poet narrates only the first seven stanzas. The remaining ones that Lermontov completed take the form of Mephistopheles's monologue at Nina's bedside. All this while, we must assume, both the poet and the reader are eavesdropping. We are already familiar with this type of structure: a brief opening narrated by the poet-author followed by an extended monologue by the hero in the presence of a mute heroine. Though Lermontov's narrative skill is greater, he is still using the same structural channels.

The monologue contains many Lermontovian staples. Mephistopheles calls the sleeping girl "My earthly angel," just as the Demon does Tamara. Like the Demon, he recalls flying about, but this time above St. Petersburg, not the Caucasus. In stanza 12, he speaks of seeing "deceit, madness, or suffering" everywhere, but he is not nearly so extravagant in his condemnation of the earth's inhabitants as was the Demon. Indeed, he smiles down at the earth like the stars.

In stanza 13 Mephistopheles describes a magnificent palace in which princes had once lived and held lavish soirees. Now it is deserted save for one old man, the lone survivor of a distinguished line, and his daughter of fourteen. The old man curses the new times, deals strictly with his servants, suffers from insomnia, and reads Voltaire.

Though the poem's structure is confusing, by this time the attentive reader begins to realize that the devil's monologue is actually a flashback. The old man's daughter is the sleeping girl to whom the monologue is addressed, though we wonder why the devil communicates with Nina in this mysterious manner. Furthermore, he is merely telling her the story of her own youth, which she presumably remembers very well.

In stanza 17 we learn that Nina "grew like a lily of the valley under glass." She is frightened by her father, and by a stern English governess. As she walks the deserted halls of the palace, she imagines herself at a magnificent ball, flirting with a dashing cavalry officer. The devil speaks of her "cunning glance," the "pretended severity of her gaze," and the smile which "snakes itself over her lips" (stanza 23). The devil has already admitted that he is in love with her, and claims that neither Raphael nor Perugino could have done justice to her profile, but the reader suspects that it is not only Nina's beauty which attracts the devil. In her he senses a kindred soul. Even as a child, he says, she was skillful at concealing her feelings. He admires her soul, the type that understands all and is ready to experience everything, "without regret, reproach, or complaint." "After all," the devil adds, "I was a little that way myself."

This poetic fragment ends as Nina reaches the "fateful" age of seventeen, when she must come out in society. Prepared for this ordeal, Nina excitedly goes to a magnificent ball. In the final stanza the devil begins to describe the ball, at which Nina attracts some notice. He takes aim at Lermontov's traditional target—high society with its pretense, artificiality, and petty spitefulness—but his tone is relatively mild.

Problems of structure and narrative stance remain unresolved in *A Fairy Tale for Children,* but its tone is balanced and integrated. The form of the narrative poem, as Lermontov himself understood, was not one that he could pursue. His future lay in prose fiction, where he made his most enduring contribution, paving the way for the great Russian psychological novels of the mid-nineteenth century through *A Hero of Our Time.*

Chapter Six
A Hero of Our Time
The Literary Background

Lermontov may claim the honor of producing the first major novel in Russian literature. Prose fiction had existed in Russia since the eighteenth century, and long prose works had been attempted during the early decades of the nineteenth century, but none of these efforts could truly be called novels.[1] The only possible exceptions to this generalization are Pushkin's "novel in verse" *Eugene Onegin,* and his long tale *The Captain's Daughter,* an imitation of the historical novels of Sir Walter Scott. In fact, the Russian reading public in the 1820s and 1830s relied heavily on translations or adaptations of foreign novels. The Reader in Lermontov's poem "Zhurnalist, chitatel, i pisatel" [The Journalist, the Reader, and the Writer, 1840] complains that most Russian prose is translated, and what Russian stories do exist attack civil servants and ridicule Moscow (1:432). As Lermontov suggests, Russians themselves produced only short stories or tales. Even these were not read by the upper aristocracy, whose members preferred contemporary French novels in the original. The old countess in Pushkin's "Pikovaya dama" [The Queen of Spades] is surprised to hear that there are such things as Russian novels.

And yet by about 1830 a new middle-class reading public was clearly beginning to emerge which demanded fiction—and prose fiction rather than verse. Pushkin himself sensed this change, and the narrator in *Eugene Onegin* speaks, only half jokingly, on two or three occasions of abandoning verse in favor of prose. His first prose work was a collection of stories, *Povesti Belkina* [The Tales of Belkin, 1831].

Lermontov also recognized the evolution in public taste, for his narrative poem *A Fairy Tale for Children* opens with the lines:

> The age of epic poems has long since passed
> And tales in verse have fallen into decline.

Old habits died hard. Nikolay Gogol in the 1830s and Ivan Turgenev in the 1840s began their literary careers with narrative poems but soon switched to prose. Gogol's collections of tales appeared in the early 1830s. At first he wrote picturesque, fantastic tales set in his native Ukraine and full of the "local color" readers wanted. Then he produced a series of very different tales, mostly set in St. Petersburg, containing many fantastic elements derived from the German writer E. T. A. Hoffman, but focusing on the ordinary lives of lowly civil servants and clerks. Gogol started the development in Russian literature of the so-called "physiological sketch," which portrayed in realistic detail the life of the urban lower classes.

Gogol's St. Petersburg tales, and also some of his stories set in the Russian provinces, deliberately presented unheroic characters in un-Romantic surroundings. But Russian readers of the 1830s liked both the adventure story set in the exotic Caucasus and the "high-society" tale.

Pushkin and Gogol initiated two important traditions in the Russian novel: the first was continued by Tolstoy and Turgenev, the second by Dostoevsky. Tolstoy and Turgenev set their novels chiefly in the countryside among the landed gentry; many of Dostoevsky's novels take place for the most part in the city of St. Petersburg and describe less fortunate members of Russian society.

But the great works of Dostoevsky, Turgenev, and Tolstoy did not begin to appear until the 1860s and even Gogol's novel *Myortvye dushi* [Dead Souls] appeared only in 1842. Therefore, when Lermontov was writing *A Hero of Our Time* in the late 1830s the novel as a genre did not really exist in Russia. It is understandable that he made at least two false starts in prose fiction before undertaking *A Hero of Our Time*. As we know, his first effort was *Vadim,* a gory tale set ostensibly during the Pugachyov Rebellion in the reign of Catherine II. His second novel was set in St. Petersburg, and also remained unfinished.

Princess Ligovskaya

Knyaginya Ligovskaya [Princess Ligovskaya] develops two main plot lines. The first involves Georges (Grigory) Pechorin, a young Hussar officer and social lion; the second conerns a poor civil servant named Stanislav Krasinsky.[2] In terms of contemporary traditions, *Princess Ligovskaya* combines the high-society tale exemplified by *Eugene Onegin* with sketches about lowly clerks in the manner of Gogol.

The two story lines are intertwined very clumsily. At the outset Pechorin's carriage knocks Krasinsky over. Later on, Pechorin visits a clerk who is working on a lawsuit in which Prince Ligovskoy is involved: he turns out to be the same Krasinsky, who has conceived a rather demonic hatred for Pechorin. Pechorin in his turn begins hating Krasinsky in an equally irrational manner. He thinks he sees Princess Ligovskaya contrasting his own plain features to the handsome countenance of Krasinsky (Chapter 8). The narrator claims that Pechorin realizes that one person does not love another for "spiritual qualities alone," and that women cannot love him truly because of his ugliness: "What to another would have been proof of the tenderest love, he despised often as signs of deceit. . . ." Pechorin resolves to triumph over these coquettes by arming himself with "sang-froid and patience," knowing that the strong always win finally over the weak, in a foreshadowing of Pechorin's musings in *A Hero of Our Time.*

Lermontov attempts third-person omniscient narration with mixed results. The narrative tone changes. On some occasions a serious narrator sympathizes with his characters; on others he makes witty asides about the foibles of society, shifts which remind us of the weaknesses of *Sashka.* The digressions account for Pechorin's life at Moscow University, his entry into cavalry school, and his service in Poland.

Princess Ligovskaya also suffers from Lermontov's inclusion of enormous amounts of dialogue designed to illustrate his own wit.

Some of the society talk is captured well, but there is too much of it. Lermontov seems to be using bits of dialogue from his play *Masquerade* while the plot comes to a standstill.

Two women figure in the novel. Pechorin's relations with Vera Ligovskaya draw upon Lermontov's feelings toward Varvara Lopukhina after her sudden marriage in 1835, and Pechorin's treatment of the unsympathetically portrayed "old maid" Liza Negurova recalls Lermontov's humiliation of Ekaterina Sushkova. The fragment breaks off as the two women are brought together.

The hopscotching plot and uneven narrative tone of *Princess Ligovskaya* are not due solely to Lermontov's youth. Apparently Lermontov and his friend Svyatoslav Raevsky worked on the story together, beginning in 1836 until early 1837, when they both were exiled from St. Petersburg. On 8 June 1838, not long after Lermontov returned to the capital, he wrote to Raevsky, then still exiled in Petrozavodsk, saying among other things the following:

The novel that you and I began has dragged on and very likely will not get finished, because the circumstances that it was based on have changed. As you know, I cannot in this case depart from the truth. (4:409)

It is reasonable to interpret this passage as meaning that the two men worked on the novel together. Since Lermontov knew nothing at firsthand about civil servants, no doubt Raevsky, who was employed as a low-ranking civil servant, could supply details about Stanislav Krasinsky (note the first name) and his life. Raevsky's contributions need not have been limited to the few episodes in which Krasinsky appears, but probably the only way to resolve the matter is to do a close textual analysis with the aid of a computer.

Lermontov's letter also provides a clue as to why the work remained unfinished. The changed circumstances of which he speaks could refer to the fact that Raevsky was no longer permitted to live in the capital. Lermontov was responsible for Raevsky's problems with the authorities, as we have seen above. Earlier in the letter he defends himself against accusations that he had tried to "get out of" something—presumably responsibility for Raev-sky's exile—as he evidently replies to charges Raevsky made in a letter that has not survived. Lermontov explains his friend's anger as stemming from "upset nerves," and goes on:

What I said was that a reply *insubordinate to the authorities* could have harmed your case while you were under arrest and that perhaps, if you had not made it, you would still be here. (Emphasis in the original.)

Lermontov does not deny his initial responsibility, but seems to argue that Raeveky could have helped his own case by being more cooperative under questioning. In these circumstances, it is un-derstandable why Lermontov should have dropped *Princess Ligov-skaya*: in the story Pechorin-Lermontov and Krasinsky-Raevsky hate each other, and its denouement would certainly have involved some tragic conflict between the two. In fact, what there is of a plot recalls several other Lermontovian works in which two men compete for the affections of a woman.

Beginnings of a Novel

Lermontov did not tell Raevsky in this letter that he was already working on another prose work. During his months in the Caucasus during 1837 Lermontov evidently conceived new ideas for a novel, or at least a series of tales. He actually did visit Taman; he traveled along the Military Georgian Highway, as does the traveling officer in the novel; and he met the man who was the model for Dr. Werner.

Lermontov was not very communicative about his writing plans, so we cannot be sure whether he had in mind originally producing a novel or merely a collection of tales. Three of the five sections comprising *A Hero of Our Time* were published sep-arately in *Otechestvennye zapiski:* "Bela. Iz zapisok ofitsera o Kav-kaze" [Bela. From the Notes of an Officer about the Caucasus] in March 1839; "The Fatalist" in November 1839; and "Taman" in February 1840. The editor appended a note to "The Fatalist" to the effect that Lermontov planned to publish a collection of his stories soon. This means that by November 1839 Lermontov already had in mind combining several stories. The manuscript was completed by February 1840 and received official censorship approval on 19 February, the day after Lermontov fought his duel against Ernest de Barante. The book appeared in May, by which time Lermontov was on his way to his second exile in the Caucasus. It was a great success, although by no means all reactions were favorable. On 6 March 1841, while on leave in St. Petersburg, he sold the rights to a second edition of the novel in 1,200 copies, the standard edition for books at that time, for 1,500 rubles (*Letopis*, 149). The second edition included the famous "Foreword."

Whatever Lermontov's initial ideas may have been, *A Hero of Our Time* appeared as a single work, a novel, not just a collection of tales.[3] The novel consists of five sections, each with its own title: "Bela," "Maksim Maksimych," "Taman," "Princess Mary," and "The Fatalist."

"Bela" is narrated by a nameless officer. While traveling in the Caucasus along the Military Georgian Highway in 1837, the officer meets an old campaigner, Maksim Maksimych. They travel on together, and Maksim Maksimych tells the story of a young officer named Grigory Pechorin who five years previously had kidnapped a Circassian princess, Bela. Bela's brother had agreed to abduct her in exchange for a marvelous horse which Pechorin stole from another Circassian, Kazbich. After her capture, Pechorin manipulates Bela into falling in love with him. The story closes when Kazbich avenges himself on Pechorin for the loss of his horse by stabbing Bela to death. Vengeance is a typical theme in Lermontov, but here it is the hero who suffers from it.

The officer and Maksim Maksimych part, but the officer is delayed at Vladikavkaz and so meets his traveling friend again in the second tale, "Maksim Maksimych." By great coincidence, Pechorin is in the same town, staying at the home of a colonel, while on his way to Persia. Maksim Maksimych rushes to see Pechorin, who treats him very coolly and departs. Thoroughly upset, Maksim Maksimych tells the officer he can have Pechorin's papers, which he was planning to return to him. Maksim Maksimych decides to stay on, but the officer leaves with his convoy.

The remaining three tales constitute "Pechorin's Journal." They are introduced by the officer, who explains that he feels free to publish them because he has recently learned that Pechorin died on his way back from Persia. Declaring his admiration for the "sincerity of this man who so mercilessly exhibited his own failings and vices" the officer continues:

The history of a human soul, be it even the meanest soul, can hardly be less curious or less instructive than the history of an entire nation— especially when it is the result of self-observation on the part of a mature mind, and when it is written without the ambitious desire to provoke sympathy or amazement. Rousseau's *Confessions* have already the defect of his having read them to his friends.[4]

Lermontov mentions Rousseau both to link his own work with Rousseau's in his reader's mind and to suggest that Pechorin's confessions will be the more genuine because they were not written for publication. Lermontov's little talk with his reader on the moral significance of his book is also important for a proper understanding of its main character. The allusion to Rousseau points up the change which has occurred in the general idea of what kinds of characters are worthy of literary portrayal.

"Taman," the first story in Pechorin's Journal, takes place around 1830 and involves a band of smugglers. A young girl, one of the band, tries to drown Pechorin after he discovers them, but he escapes and the smugglers flee.

"Princess Mary," by far the longest tale in the book, is the only one with dated entries, like a diary. It recounts Pechorin's adventures during May and June 1832 at Pyatigorsk and Kislovodsk, fashionable spas in the Russian-occupied area of the Caucasus. Irritated by Grushnitsky, a young man playing a Byronic role, Pechorin deliberately sets out to humiliate him in front of Princess Mary, whom Grushnitsky is trying to impress. Pechorin succeeds in making her fall in love with him instead, but does not respond to her. Pechorin's behavior brings him into conflict with Grushnitsky, whom he kills in a duel.

"The Fatalist," the last tale, takes place over a period of two weeks in late 1832 in a Cossack settlement. Pechorin believes he sees the signs of impending death in the face of a fellow officer, Vulich. But Vulich challenges fate by playing Russian roulette and appears to win when the pistol misfires. Later that night, however, a drunken Cossack kills Vulich and barricades himself in a building. Pechorin challenges fate in his turn by rushing the Cossack and capturing him alive.

The three sections of Pechorin's journal—"Taman," "Princess Mary," and "The Fatalist"—are arranged in chronological order. But the events described there have taken place before those recounted by the narrator in "Bela" and "Maksim Maksimych." There is in fact some slight overlap in the chronology of the diary and the first two sections, i.e., between "Bela" and "The Fatalist" (the adventure described in "The Fatalist" takes place when Pechorin is on a fortnight's leave during "Bela"). The fictional time of the novel would require that the five sections be arranged in the following order: "Taman," "Princess Mary," "The Fatalist," "Bela," and "Maksim Maksimych."

In chronological order the events of the novel take place as follows. About 1830 Pechorin is sent away from St. Petersburg to the Caucasus, probably for dueling. While en route to join his military unit, he reaches Taman and has the adventures described there. Perhaps as a reward for bravery in action, Pechorin receives a leave which he spends at Pyatigorsk in May and June 1832. After he kills Grushnitsky, Pechorin is put under Maksim Maksimych's jurisdiction at the fort described in "Bela." During the winter of 1832 Pechorin leaves the fort and spends two weeks at a Cossack settlement (*stanitsa*), where he has the experiences described in "The Fatalist." He then returns to the fort and initiates the intrigues that result in Bela's seduction and death. Some years later, in 1837, the traveling officer and Maksim Maksimych meet Pechorin at Vladikavkaz. He has apparently spent some time in St. Petersburg and is now on his way to Persia. The narrator's "Preface to Pechorin's Journal" is written a year or so later, in 1839, after news of Pechorin's death on his way back from Persia reaches St. Petersburg.

The conscious manipulation of differences between chronological time and narrative time is by now so commonplace in contemporary fiction and film (e.g., in flashbacks) that we no longer pay much attention to it. In 1840, however, this approach was fascinatingly experimental, a genuine innovation. And the distinction was still of such interest early in this century that the Russian Formalist critics expended a good deal of effort analyzing it. They introduced special terms for chronological time—the events that occur: "subject" (*syuzhet*)—and narrative time—the order in which the events are narrated: "fable" (*fabula*).

Pechorin as Hero

The sequence in which the sections of *A Hero of Our Time* are arranged has a dual advantage: it both arouses the reader's curiosity and appears to satisfy it. The work focuses upon Pechorin's personality, and the narration moves from external to internal in delineating it. "Taman" marks the transition from the external portrayal of Pechorin to his internal portrayal. Skillfully placed in the middle of the book, it forms the axis upon which the narrative pivots.

The narrator first hears about Pechorin secondhand, from Maksim Maksimych, then sees him in person and describes his physical appearance. Finally we hear Pechorin's voice directly, through his journal. Though we seem to come closer and closer to Pechorin, by the time we meet him in person in his journal, he is dead.

Lermontov did not utilize an omniscient narrator or the type of intruding narrator so common in Russian literature of that time. This marks an important difference between *A Hero of Our Time* and *Eugene Onegin*. A further distinction is that Lermontov consciously refuses to provide the reader, or the traveling officer, with any biographical information. We know practically nothing about Pechorin's background in St. Petersburg, and we can only guess why he is in the Caucasus. Here Lermontov dropped the fictional history he had given Pechorin in *Princess Ligovskaya*.

Although Lermontov originally based his hero's name upon that of the northern river Pechora, just as Onegin derives from the river Onega, there are many differences between the two "superfluous men." Onegin is passive, Pechorin, aggressive; we know more about Onegin's background, but he is shallower than Pechorin. Pushkin does not penetrate the thoughts of his hero in the same way that Lermontov does. And yet the reader, as Lermontov meant it to be, has some work to do, too. In order that Pechorin might remain something of an enigma, Lermontov created no single authoritative voice which might resolve the many puzzles remaining even after we have heard directly from Pechorin himself.

In fact Lermontov's very purpose in writing *A Hero of Our Time* has often been misunderstood. His title was certainly meant ironically. Pechorin is presented not as a model for emulation but as a warning. Lermontov makes this quite clear in his Preface to the second edition:

A Hero of Our Time, gentlemen, is indeed a portrait, but not of a single individual; it is a portrait composed of all the vices of our generation in the fullness of their development.

There is nothing new in all this. Lermontov had already written several poems (most notably "Meditation") attacking the vanity and vice of contemporary society. He openly stated his opinion of that society in *The Masquerade* through the words of the masked lady (Baroness Strahl) to Prince Zvezdich:

> You are without character, without morals, and without
>   God.
> A selfish, wicked, but weak man,
> In you alone is reflected our whole age,
> The present age which is brilliant but worthless.
> You want to lead a full life, but you avoid passion.
> You want to have everything, but you don't know
>   how to sacrifice,
> You despise people without pride and without heart,
> But you yourself are a plaything of those people. (3:274–75)

Lermontov's Preface is also quite explicit:

Our public is still so young and naive that it fails to understand a fable unless it finds a lesson at its end. It misses a humorous point and does not feel irony; it simply is badly brought up.

Lermontov here says directly that he uses irony to administer "bitter medicine, some caustic truths."

His approach was too difficult for many of his readers. In the first place, he focused his attention on one man as a representative of his generation, and what is more, on a man who was perceptively selfish. That is what his officer narrator means when he says that "the history of a human soul, be it even the meanest soul, can hardly be less curious or less instructive than the history of an entire nation." A third-person omniscient narrator could have explained Pechorin's motives, commented on them from a moral point of view, and condemned him appropriately. This might have satisfied many of Lermontov's readers. Lermontov, however, did nòt want to preach a sermon. He had higher esthetic standards by now.

The novel is composed of three first-person narratives, those of the nameless officer, Maksim Maksimych, and Pechorin.

It is interesting to see how Lermontov attempts to balance the views of the officer and Maksim Maksimych on Pechorin. The officer is depicted as a budding author seeking good material; everything is grist for his mill. He is not very sophisticated, and should not be confused with Lermontov himself. Lermontov places an ironic distance between himself and the officer when the officer muses:

"You, too are an exile," I reflected. "You wail for your wide spacious steppes! There you had room to unfurl your cold wings, while here you are stifled and cramped like an eagle that beats with cries against the bars of his iron cage." (33)

Lermontov borrows this simile from his own verse: it occurs in both *Sashka* and *The Novice*. It has been argued that the simile is intended seriously in *The Novice* and parodically in *Sashka*. I believe that in this text it is meant as a rather high-flown piece of writing by a beginning author.

The officer is delighted to find in Pechorin an almost archetypal Byronic figure. His description of Pechorin's physical appearance is very literary and mannered:

He was of medium height, a slim waist and broad shoulders testified to a sturdy constitution which was suited to bear all the hardships of a roving life and the changes of climate, and was undefeated either by the dissolution of city life or by the tempests of the soul; his dusty velvet jacket was fastened only by the two lower buttons and allowed one to see the dazzlingly clean linen which bespeaks the habits of a gentleman; his soiled gloves appeared to be made to order, so well did they fit his small aristocratic hands, and when he took off one glove I was surprised to see how thin his pale fingers were. His gait was loose and indolent, but I observed that he did not swing his arms—a sure sign of a certain reticence of nature. However, these are but my private notes based on my own observations, and by no means do I expect you to believe in them blindly. (56)

We learn also that Pechorin has fair, wavy hair, a pale brow, black moustache and eyebrows ("a sign of breeding in man, as are a black mane and a black tail in a white horse"). He also has a slightly bobbed nose, dazzlingly white teeth, and brown eyes. In short, we discover little of significance about him. His one distinctive feature is his eyes, which "never laughed when he was laughing!" The narrator qualifies his description by saying that "this bizarre trait" is "either the sign of a wicked nature or of a deep and constant melancholy" (57).

Lermontov handles his other narrator, Maksim Maksimych, with equal irony, but with an admixture of sympathy, contrasting him with the officer, who is widely read in the Byronic literature of his day. Maksim Maksimych does not read at all, and his judgments of people are quite down to earth. He represents the judgment of basic common sense upon the extravagant happenings of "Bela." Maksim Maksimych is probably a more objective witness than the officer, but Lermontov is careful not to let Maksim Maksimych dominate Pechorin.

Maksim Maksimych is pathetically upset when Pechorin does not greet him effusively as an old comrade in arms, but he should have realized by that time that Pechorin was a gloomy and formal person. Further, Maksim Maksimych attempts to establish rapport with Pechorin by asking him a series of questions culminating in: "Remember our days at the fort? Fine country for hunting! You used to be a passionate sportsman. . . . And remember Bela?" (58). The thoughtless juxtaposition of "hunting" with Bela, whom Pechorin also hunted, is unintentionally incongruous. It reminds Pechorin of the painful episode in a clumsy way, and so he retreats within himself. We sense that there is much more to Pechorin than Maksim Maksimych perceives. At the same time, we recall his comment that "you could see he [Pechorin] had been spoiled by his mamma when he was young" (42).

Lermontov had already sketched a character like Maksim Maksimych in the old soldier of his poem "Borodino." Here he expands upon that earlier outline. He does not treat Maksim Maksimych sentimentally or idealize him. Instead he creates a convincing psychological portrait of an individual totally unlike himself.

The Psychological View

The first section of Pechorin's diary, "Taman," comes as something of a surprise, even an anticlimax, for Pechorin does not come out of the episode very well. He is by no means in control of the situation and behaves rather naively, but he exhibits a sense of humor even at his own expense.

"Taman" does more than merely move our view of Pechorin from outside to inside. It shows us a pre-Byronic Pechorin, a fairly typical young officer. It is designed as a breathing space before the book's major story, "Princess Mary." Further, the story is a partial replay of "Bela," with the roles reversed: the girl is the aggressor and Pechorin the near victim. All of this occurs before the episode with Bela, by which time Pechorin has become a more demonic personality. Indeed, his attitudes have already hardened by the time of "Princess Mary," which takes place before "Bela."

"Bela" had depicted the full-fledged Pechorin at his most selfish. "Taman" does not help us understand how he got that way, for he is not reflective in this section of his journal. He hints at his future behavior and attitudes only at the end, when he writes:

What business did fate have to land me into the peaceful midst of *honest smugglers?* Like a stone thrown into the smooth water of a spring, I had disturbed their peace, and like a stone, had nearly gone to the bottom myself! (79)

This allusion to fate, as well as several other references sprinkled through "Bela" and "Princess Mary," prepares the ground for the final story, "The Fatalist."

"Princess Mary" contains a much more extensive treatment of the theme introduced in "Bela"—Pechorin's calculated attempt to conquer the heart of a woman. It is a "civilized" recasting, both in narration and setting, of the earlier story, this time in Pechorin's own words. We should remember that since the events described in "Princess Mary" precede those in "Bela," we see Pechorin in the process of formation. Futhermore, the reasons he gives for his behavior here are also valid for "Bela," and consequently it is instructive to reread "Bela" after finishing "Princess Mary."

Still, Pechorin's diary in "Princess Mary" does not resolve the enigma of his personality and behavior. It simply provides a great deal more firsthand information so that the reader may make up his own mind. In fact, in his diary Pechorin is trying to understand himself. His notes represent, as far as we can tell, his genuine feelings and thoughts—he is not posing for others since presumably he had no intention of showing the diary to anyone, much less publishing it. Nevertheless it remains simply Pechorin's view of himself, his own evaluation of his actions and motives. The few remarks made by Princess Mary and Pechorin's discarded love Vera are filtered through Pechorin's ego. It is a great pity that the traveling officer never "discovered" the diaries of either of those ladies.

Pechorin shares with Rousseau a fascination with the capricious, the inexplicable, the ambivalence of thought and behavior. A typical example of Rousseau's analytical examination of motivation is his discovery of the phenomenon of "false shame." He recalls with particular shame an immoral act—say stealing or lying—then realizes that he enjoys his feelings of remorse.

Pechorin analyzes his motivations in stealing from Grushnitsky the affections of a girl whom he cares nothing about:

Why then do I take all this trouble? Because I envy Grushnitsky? Poor thing! He has not earned it at all. Or is it the outcome of that nasty but unconquerable feeling which urges us to destroy the sweet delusions of a fellow man, in order to have the petty satisfaction of saying to him, when he asks in despair, what is it he should believe:
"My friend, the same thing happened to me, and still, you see, I dine, I sup, I sleep in perfect peace, and hope to be able to die without cries and tears." (122–23)

Pechorin's constant analysis of his own motivations is a striking feature of his journal. He has that knack, peculiar to modern heroes, of standing aside from his acting self and conducting a sort of dialogue with himself, in a tradition probably capped by Dostoevsky's *Zapiski iz podpolya* [Notes from Underground, 1864], whose dramatic monologue (*à la* Robert Browning) uses the rhetorical device of anticipating the objections and questions of his readers ("Gentlemen, you may laugh, but . . ."). Pechorin's self-analysis is offered in dated diary entries which often follow closely the events they describe. The diary form suggests authenticity, and also immediacy, a closer link between event and narration. The reader feels as though he were present as a witness at the scene. This "writing to the moment" was popularized by Samuel Richardson in his novels *Pamela* and, more especially, *Clarissa*. And like Richardson's Robert Lovelace, who pursues the luckless Clarissa for six volumes, through the longest novel in the English language, Pechorin is only happy when he can forget himself in the exercise of his will, as he triumphs over adversaries.

As the novel moves inward to become less concerned with externals, we reach what Wayne Booth has called "the inside view." From the outside, the hero may appear evil. But when one hears the villain tell his own story, things become more complex.

The twentieth century has largely ceased to view criminal behavior in moral terms; for us it has become a medical or social problem. Here too Pechorin looks forward to the twentieth century: in a confession to Princess Mary, he blames society for having made him a "moral cripple" (127). He claims that he had been a loving, trusting child, but that callous treatment had changed his character.

This confession is not only melodramatic. It is a parody of a true confession, contrived to appear Byronic and exert the maximum impact upon the listener. At the same time it contains sentiments similar to those he expresses elsewhere, during his more honest moments. After he has begun to tire of Bela, Pechorin speaks of his feelings to Maksim Maksimych. This is an honest confession, against which the false confession to Princess Mary may be measured. Here Pechorin seems to half believe all this about himself, but he will not accept responsibility for his actions. "My soul has been impaired by the fashionable world," he says. "I have a restless fancy, an insatiable heart" (41). He apparently believes that he was originally innocent, like the young soul in Lermontov's poem "Angel," and has been corrupted by society, or, as we would say now, by his environment. He despises the pretense, hypocrisy, and corruption of society; both he and Dr. Werner laugh at several particularly unedifying examples of crassness and vulgarity in Pyatigorsk.

He despises Grushnitsky, though Grushnitsky is himself a parody of Pechorin, his double in more vulgar colors. Pechorin is not amused by Grushnitsky's youthful absurdities, and he courts Princess Mary out of irritation because Grushnitshy has already laid claim to her.

Pechorin successfully captures Mary's love, then crushes her by rejecting it. In this society it was a very serious breach of decorum for a woman to make clear to a man that she cared for him before he had made her an offer of marriage. When Princess Mary is driven to ask Pechorin, "Perhaps you wish me to be the first to say that I love you?" she is doing something very daring; and when she cuts into his silence with another question, "Do you wish it?", Pechorin destroys her: " 'What for?' I answered shrugging my shoulders" (144). Princess Mary has done nothing to deserve this utterly cruel treatment, and Pechorin knows it. But he feels that society in general has injured him.

Pechorin is an extremely literary person, very well read, one who constantly thinks of himself as a character in a drama. He also insists that his acquaintances play the "roles" he has devised for them. When Dr. Werner tells him of Princess Mary's remark that Grushnitsky must have been degraded to the ranks because of a duel, Pechorin responds delightedly: "We have the beginning of a plot! . . . The denouement of this comedy will be our concern. Fate is obviously taking care of my not being bored" (95). Pechorin talks here as if he were the tool of fate, as he does also in a reflective moment before a ball when he humiliates Grushnitsky:

"Is it possible," I thought, "that my only function on earth is to ruin other people's hopes? Ever since I have lived and acted, fate has always seemed to bring me in at the denouement of other people's dramas, as if none could either die or despair without me! I am the indispensable persona in the fifth act; involuntarily, I play the miserable part of the executioner or the traitor. What could be fate's purpose in this? Might it not be that it had designated me to become the author of bourgeois tragedies and family novels, or the collaborator of some purveyor of stories for the "Library for Reading?" How should one know? How many people, in the beginning of life, think they will finish it as Alexander the Great or Lord Byron, and instead, retain for the whole of their existence, the rank of titulary counsellor?" (132–33)

This is a key quotation which contains many psychological facets of Pechorin's character. First we should note his theatrical language. He thinks that all the world's a stage, an arena in which he many exercise his will regardless of the consequences. Life is play-acting, and so is death: after he shoots Grushnitsky, who falls to the rocks below, Pechorin exclaims, "Finita la commedia!" (171). The entire passage also illuminates Pechorin's own delusions. Alexander the Great attained fame through military exploits, Byron through literature. Does Pechorin believe he has some special destiny, too?

Pechorin also speaks of vengeance, but, one may ask, vengeance against whom or what? Only in "Taman" does he suffer any sort of discomfiture at the hands of another, but why does he avenge himself on Grushnitsky? Perhaps it is because Pechorin discerns subconsciously that Grushnitsky is a parody of himself. His reactions to him are mixed. In the first place, Grushnitsky is a further example of society's pretense and superficiality; secondly, he cannot truly understand the agonizing doubts Pechorin must endure. But Grushnitsky's outlook represents an exaggeration of Pechorin's, and calls it into question by making it appear ridiculous. In crushing Grushnitsky, Pechorin is attacking himself by proxy.

Does Lermontov examine himself in dissecting Pechorin? If Pechorin is a "self" of Lermontov, he is one that Lermontov has shed. The blending of author and character that marred Lermontov's early work is absent here. The book is no *étalage du moi*, but a penetrating and critical examination of the Byronic type. A measure of the distance Lermontov has placed between himself and this type is provided by the physical descriptions in the novel. Pechorin does not resemble Lermontov physically. Grushnitsky does. Grushnitsky is Lermontov's physical twin, "well built, swarthy, and black haired" (84). The remarks Grushnitsky reportedly makes to girls recall those Lermontov made to Sushkova and Ivanova when he too was twenty-one: " 'No, you must not know this! Your pure soul would shudder! And what for? What am I to you? Would you understand me. . . .' And so forth." Further, Grushnitsky is fond of epigrams, as was Lermontov. Pechorin says of Grushnitsky that "his object is to become the hero of a novel. So often has he tried to convince others that he is a being not made for this world and doomed to suffer in secret, that he has almost succeeded in convincing himself of it" (85). This might be a description of the young Lermontov. Now Lermontov can parody his younger self, when he tried to assume the role of Byronic hero. The crucial new ingredients of *A Hero of Our Time* are psychological analysis, and the sense of an authorial presence, distinct from the hero, which judges him objectively. Pechorin is a "Byronic" hero, but set in perspective by a *reductio ad absurdum* of the type: Grushnitsky.

The Philosophy of a Hero

Lermontov's analysis of Pechorin's complex character has re-
verberated throughout the nineteenth and twentieth centuries.
Pechorin recognizes the emptiness of society's moral codes, but
he adheres to a form of philosophical nihilism: he can find no
ground of action other than his own will. Pechorin mercilessly
strips the Byronic glamour from himself and acknowledges his
own selfishness, ambition, and desire for power:

I look upon the sufferings and joys of others only in relation to myself
as on the food sustaining the strength of my soul. I am no longer
capable myself of frenzy under the influence of passion: ambition with
me has been suppressed by circumstances, but it has manifested itself
in another form, since ambition is nothing else than thirst for power,
and my main pleasure—which is to subjugate to my will all that
surrounds me, and to excite the emotions of love, devotion, and fear
in relation to me—is it not the main sign and greatest triumph of
power? To be to somebody the cause of sufferings and joys, without
having any positive right to it—is this not the sweetest possible nour-
ishment for our pride? (123)

Pechorin finally emerges as a pale reflection of Napoleon, a
man reduced to tricking people. Pechorin needs others so that
he may exercise his will over them. He is not a solitary rebel,
or a loner at all. He must attract people to himself in order to
reject them. He is in fact a parasite who feeds on other people.
The images of food and eating in this passage pick up the metaphor buried in Pechorin's remark in "Princess Mary" that he
understands the vampire (145).

Lermontov has laid bare the contradictions in the Byronic hero
that actually make Pechorin a victim of himself. He tells us he
can never abandon his "freedom" for the commitment of marriage,
and yet he is not free. He is obsessed by the idea of exercising
his will over others to make them unhappy. Such a man is a
prisoner of his own will.

If the philosophical element in the novel were not so important,
Lermontov might well have ended it after "Princess Mary," although it could be argued that structurally the novel needs a fifth

section to act as a sort of coda after the passion and excitement of "Princess Mary." It is tempting to compare the five parts of *A Hero of Our Time* to the five acts of a tragedy, and one need not press such a comparison too far to see that "Princess Mary," the most important section of the novel, like the fourth act of a tragedy, requires some final section as a conclusion.

Since "The Fatalist" overlaps chronologically with "Bela," Lermontov returns us to the beginning, as he does so often in his lyrics, repeating a refrain or line(s) in the final stanza. The great care that Lermontov took with his short poems should alert us to the possibility that "The Fatalist" may be of prime significance for the entire novel. We have already discussed the possible "psychological" reasons for the arrangement of the novel's five sections. Now we need to assess the "philosophical" reasons for that arrangement.

Two key words in *Hero* are "fate" and "will." The word "fate" is used at regular intervals throughout the novel, and by all three narrators, but it occurs most frequently in statements attributed to Pechorin or comments he makes directly in his diary. The word "will" (*volya*) occurs less frequently, and in disguised form, in compounds and cognates. Pechorin's quarrel is with existence, and not simply with social conventions. He seeks justification for his actions in the concept of fate or predestination. His experiences lead him to conclude—and the episode in "The Fatalist" confirms that belief—that fate determines our existence.

Pechorin sees death in Vulich's face. He is convinced that Vulich will die that night, and he is disconcerted when Vulich survives his game of Russian roulette. Vulich's death a short time later at the hands of the drunken Cossack reassures Pechorin. His belief in fate, or predestination, helps explain his own courage: a man will die only when he is destined to, and before then it does not really matter if one exposes oneself to danger.

But Pechorin's concept of fate also weights the scales in favor of free will and against responsibility. Pechorin is a precursor of Ivan Karamazov. He decides that it makes no difference whether we do good or evil if everything is predestined. He anticipates

Nietzsche in seeking to validate his existence by testing his will under a variety of circumstances.

In "The Fatalist" Lermontov sums up the major theme of the novel and provides the reader with an important clue to Pechorin's behavior. Brilliant though he is, Pechorin has argued himself into a false sense of security. His uncertainty in "The Fatalist" about the validity of fate as a guide to action shows that he is still not entirely convinced of his theory. Presumably he finds its confirmation in Bela's death when he returns to the fort and Maksim Maksimych.

The fact that Lermontov can penetrate so deeply into the essence of the Byronic type by which he had once been so dazzled is a measure of his artistic maturity when he wrote *A Hero of Our Time*. Pechorin exercises his free will when that suits him, and ascribes his actions to fate in other cases. This is no way to live. Lermontov has analyzed the social and psychological disease represented by the Byronic hero, and has applied, with consummate skill, a "bitter medicine, some caustic truth."

Chapter Seven
Lermontov and Posterity

Lermontov's Legacy

Lermontov left a remarkable legacy for one who died so young. Scholars have traced echoes of his poetry in the works of later Russian poets, and such men as Alexander Blok and Boris Pasternak greatly admired him as a poet.[1] He made his greatest impact on Russian literature as a prose writer, however. Gogol was perceptive when he told his friend Sergey Aksakov that Lermontov would be a greater novelist than a poet. Had Lermontov lived longer, that might easily have been the case.

Tolstoy, Dostoevsky, and Chekhov were all influenced by Lermontov's prose. Tolstoy's descriptions of the Caucasus, his battle scenes, his satire against high society, all go back to Lermontov. Dostoevsky developed Lermontov's antihero and his interest in metaphysical questions.[2] Both Tolstoy and Dostoevsky carried the psychological novel initiated by Lermontov to perfection. For Chekhov Lermontov was the great stylist, the writer of perfect stories.

Vladimir Fisher argues that toward the end of his life Lermontov had worked out his own style, the "best in Russian literature." "In comparison," he says, "Pushkin is archaic, Turgenev prosaic, Tolstoy and Dostoevsky ponderous, and Gogol incorrect."[3]

As Lermontov matured he gained a fuller perception of his own dilemma and that of his generation. Pechorin was designed to shock the reading public into a recognition of the malady threatening to destroy Russian society.

I believe that Lermontov had completely fathomed the impact of the Byronic hero and its ultimate contradictions by the time he wrote his novel. The later emanations of the Byronic type continued well into the twentieth century, and their power and glamour were not so well understood by later generations. In his study *L'Homme révolté* [The Rebel, 1951], Albert Camus attempts to analyze the causes of state terrorism in Nazi Germany and Stalinist Russia by tracing the development since the eighteenth century of metaphysical rebellion, or what he calls "le crime logique" as opposed to "le crime de passion." Camus sees the history of the last two centuries as "the history of European pride." He traces that history through Milton's Satan, the Marquis de Sade, the Byronic hero (he refers to "the Romantic hero" and "the revolt of the dandies"), nihilism, and Dostoevsky's Ivan Karamazov to twentieth-century dictators who argue that individuals may be killed if need be in order to create a glorious future for all mankind.

It is of some interest that Camus quotes Lermontov rather than Byron, and finds in the Romantic period the beginnings of a fatal confusion between good and evil:

In order to combat evil, the rebel, because he judges himself innocent, renounces good and creates evil once again. The Romantic hero introduces the profound and, one might say, religious confusion between good and evil.[4]

The hero is outraged by injustice and by his inability to right the wrongs he sees around him: "The romantic hero feels compelled to do evil by his nostalgia for an unrealizable good. His excuse is sorrow." This formulation tells us much both about Lermontov himself and his hero.

Lermontov and Politics

Lermontov had the misfortune to grow up in the reign of Nicholas I. Young men like him belonged to a "lost generation" of the 1830s, a time when the exhilaration created by the French Revolution in Europe and the early liberal years of Alexander I's reign in Russia had been crushed. In fact, there is an interesting parallel between the mood in Russia and the gloom that pervaded

French thought and literature after the restoration of the Bourbons in 1815. It is no accident that Byronism and the cult of Napoleon as romanticized liberator were most popular in France and Russia. The sociopolitical atmosphere in both countries was hospitable to the rebellious outsider who despaired of finding a constructive outlet for his talents.[5]

The exact nature of Lermontov's political beliefs, as of his personality in general, has long been a matter of great controversy. During the nineteenth century, conservatives regarded him as a moral outcast: his own behavior and that of his hero Pechorin brought disrepute to the good name of Russia. Soviet scholars, for quite understandable reasons, have sought by and large to demonstrate that Lermontov was really a political liberal, if not a closet revolutionary.

I have tried to show that this latter view cannot be sustained by the facts. Lermontov had an aristocrat's distaste for the herd. He was never a joiner, and all his instincts militated against association with such men as Alexander Herzen and other liberals of the time. Even in the 1830s, when he was out of favor with the authorities, Lermontov refused to engage in serious political discussions with the Decembrist exiles he met in the Caucasus. For example, Mikhail Nazimov recalls engaging in wide-ranging conversations with the poet but becoming irritated because he seemingly had no firm beliefs and refused to take reform proposals seriously. When Nazimov upbraided him for his flippancy and asked him for his evaluation of contemporary youth, Lermontov mockingly replied: "We have no direction at all; we just meet, have a good time, make our careers, and chase after women" (*Vosp.*, 516). As often as not their conversations ended with Nazimov upset and Lermontov enjoying his discomfort.

Far from being a political liberal, Lermontov was rather close to the Slavophile outlook, a point well made by V. D. Spasovich and developed in 1914 by N. L. Brodsky, who emphasizes the personal ties between Lermontov and the Slavophiles Vladimir Odoevsky, Aleksey Khomyakov, and Yury Samarin.[6]

Lermontov and Literature

Lermontov's literary views are even more difficult to define. He was not a man of letters and never belonged to any literary groupings. Not much of his correspondence has survived, and what there is of it has little to say about literature. We do not have his library, and we do not know what he read, except for a few references in his poetry and prose. He wrote no literary criticism.

Orthodox Soviet critics have a ready-made framework into which they try to squeeze Lermontov. The literary equivalent of a political liberal or revolutionary is a Realist, so they bend every effort to show that Lermontov is a Realist. Much Soviet criticism on Lermontov is given over to the question of whether he moved from Romanticism to Realism or remained a Romantic to the end. Such a late prose character sketch as "Kavkazets" [The Caucasian], some maintain, marks Lermontov's advance along the "road to Realism." If so, what are we to make of the Romantic "Shtoss," written after "The Caucasian"?

It makes as little sense to term Lermontov a Realist as it is to call Gogol a Realist. For one thing, until the very end of his life, Lermontov continued to write poetry which dealt with the same subjects he had treated at the beginning. The crucial difference was that from 1837 on Lermontov wrote with vastly superior artistry. Both his prose and his poetry continued to be autobiographical, but now he probed more deeply and completely controlled his materials. It is clear also that Lermontov looked back coolly at his earlier Byronic enthusiasms. This new maturity is obvious in *A Hero of Our Time,* and also in his album verses "Lyubil i ya v bylye gody" [I Too Loved in Years Gone By], where he says he is now bored with the "noisy storms of nature" and the "secret storms of passions" described in "incoherent and deafening language" (1:469).

No one can say how Lermontov might have developed as a writer. Like John Keats, who also died very young, Lermontov underwent a relatively long period of apprenticeship and displayed the same astonishing "self-corrective growth" demonstrated by Keats.[7] It comes as a shock to realize that in speaking of Lermontov's mature period we are referrring to works he wrote between the ages of twenty-two and twenty-six. If Dostoevsky and Tolstoy had died at the same age as Lermontov, they would scarcely merit a footnote in the history of Russian literature.

Dmitry Merezhkovsky once wrote that "Pushkin is the diurnal luminary and Lermontov the nocturnal luminary of Russian poetry."[8] Halley's Comet flashed across the night sky of St. Petersburg on 13 November 1835, not long before Lermontov began his public career as a writer.[9] Perhaps the metaphor of the comet best captures the impression he made upon his contemporaries and on later generations: brilliant but alarming, fleeting but unforgettable.

Notes and References

Chapter One

1. Russian scholars state that although Lermontov's Spanish ancestry is imagined, he actually was descended from a Scottish soldier-of-fortune who entered Russian service early in the seventeenth century. See genealogical tree in V. A. Manuilov, *Lermontovskaia Entsiklopediia* (Moscow, 1981). Genealogical tree is given between pp. 464, 465. See also pp. 467–68.

2. M. Iu. Lermontov, *Sobranie sochinenii v chetyrëkh tomakh,* [Collected Works in Four Volumes], 2d. rev. ed. (Leningrad, 1979), 1:217. Future references to Lermontov's works in this edition will be given in the text by volume and page number in parentheses.

3. M. I. Gillel'son and V. A. Manuilov, eds., *M. Iu. Lermontov v vospominaniiakh sovremennikov* [M. Iu. Lermontov in the Memoirs of His Contemporaries] (Moscow, 1972), p. 33. Shan-Girei comes across in his memoirs as a sensible, uncomplicated man who was very fond of the poet, but did not fully understand the complexities of his personality. Nevertheless, his memoirs are based on a close acquaintance with Lermontov over several years and remain one of our best sources. Future references to the Gillel'son and Manuilov edition of memoirs will be given in the text as *Vosp.* followed by page number.

4. V. A. Manuilov, ed., *Letopis' zhizni i tvorchestva M. Iu. Lermontova* [Chronology of the Life and Work of M. Iu. Lermontov] (Moscow-Leningrad, 1964), p. 35. Future references to this detailed chronology of Lermontov's life and works will be given in the text as *Letopis* with page number.

5. This was Lermontov's view throughout his life. Later on, according to Herzen's great friend and collaborator Nikolai Ogarëv, Lermontov described discussion groups as "masturbation." Quoted in Lidia Ginzburg, *Tvorcheskii put' Lermontova* [Lermontov's Creative Path] (Leningrad, 1940), p. 28.

6. Indulging in some homespun psychoanalysis, Dostoevskii concluded that both Byron and Lermontov wrote and behaved as they did because of physical defects. In his notebooks, written during the last

twenty years of his life, Dostoevskii often links the two together in a most uncomplimentary way: "The reason for Cain is that Byron was lame; the reason for Lermontov's attitudes is that he was so ugly." See "Neizdannyi Dostoevskii" [Unpublished Dostoevskii], *Literaturnoe nasledstvo* [Literary Heritage] 83 (Moscow, 1971):375.

7. The Hussar poems have little literary merit, and one need not regret their omission from recent Soviet editions. They do appear, with prudish cuts, in the Academia edition of 1935–37.

8. Only extracts are given in *Sob. soch.*, vol. 1. For the full text of Lermontov's statement see the Academia edition of his works (1936), 2:177–79.

9. Rostopchina, who later became a well-known poet herself, in 1858 wrote a sketch of Lermontov's life for the French writer Alexandre Dumas–père. As an example of Lermontov's playful character and high spirits during his last leave, she recalls a prank he played on his friends. He told them he would give a reading of a new novel which would last at least four hours, and he insisted that all doors be locked. He then read a short, fantastic tale in the style of Hoffmann and Gogol which took only about fifteen minutes. This is the story published under the title "Shtoss," beginning "There was a musical evening at the home of Count V . . ." (see Rostopchina's letter in *Vosp.*, 285). One should not draw too many conclusions from this unfinished piece, but it does demonstrate that Lermontov was well read in the "fantastic realism" of his time, especially the St. Petersburg tales of Gogol. D. S. Merezhkovskii and others have argued that "Shtoss" influenced Dostoevskii. See also two fine articles: I. S. Chistova, "Prozaicheskii otryvok M. Iu. Lermontova 'Shtoss' i 'natural'naia' povest' 1840-kh godov" [Lermontov's Prose Fragment "Shtoss" and the "Natural" Tale of the 1840s], *Russkaia literatura* [Russian Literature], no. 1 (1972):116–22; and V. E. Vatsuro, "Posledniaia povest' Lermontova" [Lermontov's Last Tale], in *M. Iu. Lermontov: Issledovaniia i materialy* [M. Iu. Lermontov: Articles and Materials] (Leningrad, 1979), pp. 223–52.

10. The point must be emphasized because some American scholars have uncritically accepted the claim that Lermontov was pursued to his death by a conspiracy headed by the Tsar. See, for example, John Mersereau, Jr., *Mikhail Lermontov* (Carbondale, Ill., 1962), p. 20. For details on Lermontov's last exile and final duel see Helen Michailoff, "The Death of Lermontov (The Poet and the Tsar)," *Russian Literature Triquarterly*, no. 10 (1974) pp. 279–97.

11. In fairness it must be stated that leading Lermontov scholars in the Soviet Union now declare that suggestions of a conspiracy, headed

by the Tsar or not, are completely without foundation. See *Lermontov-skaia Entsiklopediia*, p. 151.

12. An interesting, if severe, moral indictment of Lermontov is given by the Russian philosopher Vladimir Solov'ëv in an article in *Vestnik Evropy* [Herald of Europe] for February 1901. Iakov Kostenetskii reports in his memoirs that he got a bad impression of Lermontov in 1841 as a social snob and member of an aristocratic clique who looked down on other officers not belonging to his circle.

13. In his last letters Lermontov displays a touching fear that he may be forgotten by his friends. In September 1840 he wrote to Aleksei Lopukhin: "You cannot imagine how painful it is to think that our friends have forgotten us." On 22 May 1841 he wrote to Sophia Karamzina (in French): "Stay well, be happy, and do not forget me."

14. A. Golubev, *Kniaz' A. I. Vasil'chikov* [Prince A. I. Vasil'chikov] (St. Petersburg, 1882), p. 39. See also the newspaper *Nabliudatel'* [Observer], no. 1, 1881, as quoted in Emma Gershtein, *Sud'ba Lermontova* [Lermontov's Fate] (Moscow: Sovetskii Pisatel', 1964). Laurence Kelly, *Lermontov: Tragedy in the Caucasus* (New York: Braziller, 1978) reports Lermontov's last words with the absurd claim that this is a new discovery in Lermontov scholarship when in fact they have been known for a century.

Chapter Two

1. David Perkins, ed., *English Romantic Writers* (New York: Harcourt, Brace & World, 1967), p. 782.

2. Lermontov began to study English in 1829 with an English tutor. He continued to study English at Moscow University, and in the fall of 1831 attended a series of lectures by one Edward Harvey in which "selections from the works of Lord Byron, Walter Scott, and Thomas Moore were read with critical analysis and explanations" (*Letopis'*, 40).

3. The notebooks have not been published. Most are preserved in the Institute of Russian Literature (Pushkinskii Dom) in Leningrad, and the remainder at the Saltykov-Shchedrin Public Library, also in Leningrad.

4. B. M. Eikhenbaum, *Stat'i o Lermontove* [Articles on Lermontov] (Moscow-Leningrad, 1961), p. 13. I have expanded and adapted Eikhenbaum's list, which refers to Lermontov's 1829 notebook of poems.

5. The narrative poems are given in *Sob. soch.* vol 2.

6. See Robin Feuer Miller, "Dostoevsky and the Tale of Terror," in John Garrard, ed., *The Russian Novel from Pushkin to Pasternak* (New Haven: Yale University Press, 1983).

7. M. E. Duchesne, *Michel Iouriévitch Lermontov: Sa vie et ses oeuvres* (Paris, 1910), p. 333.

8. An exception is "Rusalka" [The Water Nymph], a poem in the folk style that Lermontov published in 1839 and included in his collection of 1840, where it is dated 1836.

9. In rhyme schemes, lower case indicates feminine rhymes, and upper case masculine rhymes.

Chapter Three

1. The text of the play is in *Sob. soch.*, 3:258–380.

Chapter Four

1. In typically shotgun fashion Dmitrii Merezhkovskii remarked that "all Lermontov's poetry is a recollection of this song heard in past eternity" (referring to the song Lermontov recalled his mother singing to him as a small child). The Merezhkovskii statement occurs in his booklet *Lermontov: Poet sverkhchelovechestva* [Lermontov: Poet of Superhumanity] (St. Petersburg: Prosveshchenie, 1911), p. 21. Vladimir Fisher developed this idea in his "Poetika Lermontova" [Lermontov's Poetics], *Venok M. Iu. Lermontovu* [A Garland for Lermontov] (Moscow-Petrograd, 1914), pp. 200–202. To this I might add that the old servant Annushka repeats the account of the mother singing a sad song to a child in *The Strange Man*, 1:3. Early poems celebrating the power of music may be found in *Sob. soch.*, 1:261, 267.

2. Fisher, "Poetika Lermontova," pp. 222–23.

3. The Soviet scholar D. E. Maksimov also states that "the essential feature of Lermontov's lyrics rests in their combination of civic [*grazhdanskii*], philosophical and personal content." See his *Poeziia Lermontova* [Lermontov's Poetry] (Moscow-Leningrad, 1964), p. 31. He later suggests (p. 59), however, that "philosophy" is more characteristic of Lermontov's juvenilia, and he argues convincingly that Eikhenbaum has exaggerated the influence of systematic philosophers like Schelling on Lermontov's poetry.

4. The texts of Lermontov's lyrics may be found in *Sob. soch.*, vol. 1. References are given in the text. Translations throughout are mine.

5. In an interesting analysis Eikhenbaum contrasts the poem to one by Afanasii Fet and tries to prove that Lermontov's lyric possesses an

intonational and rhythmic structure established without reference to logic or the meaning of the words. See his "Melodika russkogo liricheskogo stikha" [Melodic Features in the Russian Lyric] in *O poezii* [On Poetry] (Leningrad, 1969), pp. 420–31.

6. There is a fascinating analysis of this poem by the leading Soviet structuralist Iurii Lotman in his book *Analiz poeticheskogo teksta* [Analysis of the Poetic Text] (Leningrad: Prosveshchenie, 1972), pp. 169–79. Lotman seeks the hidden meaning of the poem by examining the interplay between the pronouns "I" and "you." He suggests that Lermontov reveals a typically Romantic ambivalence toward the beloved, since in loving her the poet must cease in some measure to love himself and thus deny the primacy of the self.

7. Fisher, "Poetika Lermontova," p. 226, suggests that Lermontov learned to write such allegories from Heinrich Heine, with whom he had much in common, but took this type of poem far beyond anything Heine achieved.

Chapter Five

1. Texts of Lermontov's narrative poems are given in *Sob. Soch.* vol. 2. All translations are mine.

2. Duchesne, *Lermontov*, pp. 127–28.

3. See the helpful discussion in V. E. Vatsuro, "K tsenzurnoi istorii *Demona*" [*The Demon* and the Censorship], in *M. Iu. Lermontov: Issledovaniia i materialy*, pp. 410–14.

4. Duchesne, *Lermontov*, p. 138.

5. In the following discussion I have drawn upon comments by my colleague, Natalie Moyle.

Chapter Six

1. For a discussion of eighteenth-century efforts to write prose fiction in Russia, see J. G. Garrard, *Mixail Čulkov* (Mouton: The Hague and Paris, 1970).

2. The text of *Princess Ligovskaya* is printed in *Sob. soch.*, 4:110–70.

3. Fisher, "Poetika Lermontova," p. 233, thinks that the parts are only "weakly welded together." I disagree. In "Taman" and "The Fatalist" Fisher sees the author's "total freedom in his relation to the characters described." He also notes the special dramatic interest of "Princess Mary," which he feels anticipates Dostoevsky. He is critical of "Maksim Maksimych" on the grounds that the old soldier and the

overly elegant narration do not match: "What is appropriate in a Romantic poem like *The Novice* becomes risky in a novel."

4. Russian text is printed in *Sob. soch.*, 4:183–314. Page references in my text are to the Nabokov translation.

Chapter Seven

1. For a survey of Lermontov's influence on nineteenth-century Russian poetry see I. N. Rozanov, "Otzvuki Lermontova" [Echoes of Lermontov], in *Venok M. Iu. Lermontovu* [Garland for Lermontov], (1914), pp. 237–79. The second part of Rozanov's article, pp. 279–89, deals with a few imitators of *A Hero of Our Time*, more particularly of Pechorin.

Alexander Blok felt a special kinship with Lermontov, and similarities between them have often been noted. Boris Pasternak dedicated his *Sestra moia zhizn'* [My Sister Life] (1922) to Lermontov and considered his work a model for the embodiment of the personality in poetry.

Osip Mandelshtam's poem "Grifel'naia oda" [Slate Ode] looks back not only to Derzhavin but also to Lermontov's "Vykhozhu odin ia na dorogu" [I Go Out Alone onto the Road]. See Victor Terras, "The Time Philosophy of Osip Mandel'shtam," *Slavonic and East European Review* 47 (1969):344–54; and Jennifer Baines, "Mandel'shtam's 'Grifelnaia oda'," *Oxford Slavonic Papers* 5 (1972):61–82.

2. Merezhkovsky discussed the links between Lermontov and .the two later novelists in his *Lermontov: Poet sverkhchelovechestva*, pp. 46, 50–51. Tolstoy once said that "Borodino" inspired him to write *War and Peace*.

3. Fisher, "Poetika Lermontova," p. 214. Fisher detects three basic "manners" or "styles" in Lermontov's works: exotic-Byronic, which culminates in *The Demon* and *The Novice*, but which Lermontov was abandoning toward the end of his life; popular or folk (*narodnyi*), best exemplified in *Kalashnikov*, though this is an isolated work, and the style could lead nowhere; and realistic and satirical (*real'no-satiricheskii*), which runs parallel with the first two, for example, in epigrams, the Hussar poems, and *The Tambov Treasurer's Wife*. Fisher argues that this third style owes more to Pushkin than to Byron; it requires observation and wit rather than imagination. At the end of his life, Fisher claims, Lermontov began to blend all three styles into one.

4. Albert Camus, *L'Homme révolté* (Paris: Gallimard, 1951), p. 68. In 1911 Merezhkovsky.said that "Lermontov was the first in Russian literature to raise the religious question of evil" (36).

5. For a detailed examination of the parallels between the French and Russian Romantic movements see J. G. Garrard, "Karamzin, Mme de Staël, and the Russian Romantics," *American Contributions to the Seventh International Congress of Slavists* (The Hague and Paris: Mouton, 1974), pp. 221–46.

6. N. L. Brodskii, "Poeticheskaia ispoved' russkogo intelligenta 30–40-kh godov" [Poetic Confession of a Russian Intellectual of the 1830s and 1840s] *Venok M. Iu. Lermontovu*, pp. 100–108.

7. Perkins, *English Romantic Writers*, p. 1120.

8. Merezhkovskii, *Lermontov: Poet sverkhchelovechestva*, p. 5.

9. Lermontov refers to Halley's Comet twice in *Sashka*, in stanzas 47 and 127. Sashka's aunt is afraid that the comet signals the end of the world.

Selected Bibliography

PRIMARY SOURCES

1. Russian

Bibliografiia literatury o M. Iu. Lermontove: 1917–77. Compiled by
O. V. Miller. Leningrad: "Nauka," 1980. Excellent and very
thorough, although limited to Soviet, chiefly Russian, materials
for the period indicated. Includes everything written about Lermontov, even items on art, music, film, and television. Fully
indexed.

Geroi nashego vremeni. Edited by B. M. Eikhenbaum and E. E. Naidich.
Moscow: "Literaturnye pamiatniki," 1962. Excellent edition with
very good introduction and notes.

Polnoe sobranie sochinenii v piati tomakh. Edited by Boris Eikenbaum et
al. Moscow-Leningrad: "Academia," 1935–37. Gives all variant
texts and manuscripts, and full annotations. Remains the best
edition, but should be checked against the following for recent
discoveries and modification of some hypotheses.

Polnoe sobranie sochinenii v shesti tomakh. Edited by N. F. Bel'chikov,
B. P. Gorodetskii, and B. V. Tomashevskii. Moscow-Leningrad:
Academy of Sciences of the USSR, 1954–57. Basically a reprint
of the "Academia" edition , but omits the "Hussar poems" altogether. Sometimes the notes are less informative, sometimes they
contain more complete texts of archival materials.

Sobranie sochinenii v chetyrëkh tomakh. Edited by V. A. Manuilov et al.
2d rev. ed. Leningrad: "Nauka," 1979–81. I have given references
to this edition in my text for the convenience of the reader since
it is easily obtained in the West at this time. The notes, however,
are not nearly as full as in the previous editions cited. Furthermore,
the interpretations are sometimes subject to political bias. It remains a useful edition, if approached with caution.

Gillel'son, Iu. I., and Manuilov, V. A., eds. *M. Iu. Lermontov v vospominaniiakh sovremennikov.* Moscow: Khudozhestvennaia literatura,

1972. Valuable collection of materials, with useful notes on memoirists and correction of obvious errors in dates, etc.

Manuilov, V. A., ed. *Letopis' zhizni i tvorchestva M. Iu. Lermontova.*
Moscow-Leningrad: "Nauka," 1964. Indispensable day-by-day
record of Lermontov's life, with extensive quotations from archival
materials, memoirs, etc.

Viskovatyi, P. A. *Mikhail Iurievich Lermontov: zhizn' i tvorchestvo.* Mos-
cow, 1891. Vol. 6 of Viskovatyi's edition of Lermontov's works.
Contains some errors, hearsay, and questionable hypotheses.
Nevertheless, a major source for Lemontov's biography.

Iu. G. Oksman, ed., *Sushkova (Khvostova), E. A. Zapiski. 1812–1841.*
Leningrad: "Academia," 1928. Only complete edition.

2. English

The reader without Russian has been well served with translations of
A Hero of Our Time, but the situation with Lermontov's poetry is far
less satisfactory.

The Demon and Other Poems. Translated by Eugene M. Kayden. Yellow
Springs, Ohio: The Antioch Press, 1965. Ignore the introduction
by Sir Maurice Bowra, which is full of uninformed waffling. The
selection is good, and the translations attempt to reproduce the
meter (sometimes) and rhyme of the verse, with mixed reşults.
Superior to the Daniels and L'Ami and Welikotny translations.

A Hero of Our Time. Translated by Paul Foote. Harmondsworth: Penguin
Books, 1966. With introduction but no notes.

A Hero of Our Time. Translated by Vladimir Nabokov in collaboration
with Dmitri Nabokov. New York: Doubleday Anchor, 1958.
Useful introduction and notes. I have used this edition for references in English.

A Lermontov Reader. Translated by Guy Daniels. New York: Macmillan,
1965. A silly, opinionated introduction is followed by a capricious
selection of lyrics, but the translations are sometimes quite good.
Does include *Princess Ligovskaia* and *A Strange One* (i.e., *Strannyi
chelovek*).

"Masquerade." Translated into prose by Roger W. Phillips. In *Russian
Literature Triquarterly,* no. 7 (Fall 1973):68–117. Useful, but with
occasional infelicities and errors.

Michael Lermontov. Translated by C. E. L'Ami and Alexander Welikotny.
Winnipeg: University of Manitoba Press, 1967. The long biography should be treated with great caution. The translations are
evidently a labor of love, but are clumsy and contain errors. The

fullest collection of Lermontov's verse available in English; includes "Sashka," "Izmail Bey," and the play *Two Brothers*.

Selected Works. Moscow: Progress Publishers, 1976. Ignore the orthodox Soviet foreword. The book is well produced and illustrated with color plates. The selection is very good, including major lyrics and narrative poems, as well as *A Hero*. Translations generally sound, especially those by Avril Pyman, the British specialist on Alexander Blok.

SECONDARY SOURCES

1. Books and Articles in Books

Brik, O. M. "Zvukovye povtory: Analiz zvukovoi struktury stikha." In *Sborniki po teorii poeticheskogo iazyka* (Petrograd, 1917), 2:24–62. Reprinted in *Poetika,* nos. 1–2 (Petrograd, 1919):58–98. Suggestive insights into the poetic technique of Pushkin and Lermontov; influential in writings of Eikenbaum and many others.

Duchesne, M. E. *Michel Iouriévitch Lermontov: sa vie et ses oeuvres*. Paris: Plon-Nourrit, 1910. A doctoral dissertation; plot summaries with minimal explication. Dated, but valuable for its review of English, French, and German influences in Lermontov's works. This latter portion translated into Russian and still widely used by Soviet scholars: E. Duchesne, *Poeziia M. Iu. Lermontova v eë otnoshenii k vusskoi i zapadnoevropeiskim literaturam* (Kazan': M. A. Golubev, 1914).

Eikhenbaum, B. *Lermontov: Opyt istoriko-literaturnoi otsenki*. Leningrad: Gos. izdatel'stvo, 1924. Reprinted in "Slavische Propyläen" series (Munich: Wilhelm Fink Verlag, 1967) and translated into English by Ray Parrott and Harry Weber (Ann Arbor, Mich.: Ardis, 1981). Generally ignored and never reprinted in the Soviet Union because of its "formalism"; widely admired in the West for the same reason. Still valuable, chiefly for placing Lêrmontov in Russian literature of his time and for developing important insights of Vladimir Fisher.

Eikhenbaum, Boris. *Melodika russkogo liricheskogo stikha*. Petrograd: "Opoiaz," 1922. Reprinted in B. Eikhenbaum, *O poezii*. Leningrad: Sovetskii pisatel', 1969. Contains a suggestive short section on Lermontov.

Fisher, Vladimir. "Poetika Lermontova." In *Venok M. Iu. Lermontovu: Iubyleinyi sbornik*. Moscow-Petrograd, 1914, pp. 196–236. By far the best study of Lermontov's works in any language. Seminal influence on the writings of Boris Eikhenbaum. *Venok* is also the best single volume of articles on Lermontov. Unfortunately, never reprinted.

Garrard, John. "Old Wine in New Bottles: The Legacy of Lermontov." In *Poetika Slavica: Studies in Honour of Zbigniew Folejewski.* Ottawa, Canada: University of Ottawa Press, 1981, pp. 41–52. An examination of Lermontov's role in the rise of the Russian novel.

Ginzburg, Lidia. *Tvorcheskii put' Lermontova.* Leningrad: Khud. literatura, 1940. Sensible and thoughtful; more balanced appraisal than in Eikhenbaum's better-known 1924 book. See also sections on Lermontov in her books *O lirike* (Moscow-Leningrad: Sovetskii pisatel', 1964) and *O psikhologicheskoi proze* (Leningrad: Sov. pisatel', 1971).

Goscilo, Helena Irena. "From Dissolution to Synthesis: The Use of Genre in Lermontov's Prose." Ph.D. dissertation, Indiana University, 1976. A more sophisticated analysis than in Mersereau, but sometimes insights get lost in a welter of references to extraneous material and authors.

Iakovlev, M. A. *M. Iu..Lermontov kak dramaturg.* Leningrad: "Kniga," 1924. Thorough and helpful review of Lermontov's plays: their autobiographical features, social content, and reflection of foreign and domestic influences.

Kelly, Laurence. *Lermontov: Tragedy in the Caucasus.* New York: Braziller, 1978. Originally published in 1977 in England; not a book about Lermontov as a writer, but a popular biography and travelogue dressed up with reference notes and bibliography. Kelly's knowledge of Russian language and literature is unsteady, but he makes an amiable companion through the Caucasus, which obviously interests him a good deal more than does Lermontov. Handsomely illustrated.

Lavrin, Janko. *Lermontov.* New York: Hillary House, 1959. The only book in English on the life and works; a brief outline (100 pages), but well written and informed. Superior to Duchesne, Goscilo, Kelly, Mersereau, and Turner.

Maksimov, D. E. *Poeziia Lermontova.* Moscow-Leningrad: "Nauka," 1964. A mixed bag, but many sensible pages, notably on "Mtsyri" and the relationship between Lermontov and Blok.

Manuilov, V. A. *Geroi nashego vremeni: Kommentarii.* Moscow-Leningrad: "Prosveshchenie," 1966. Typically thorough and balanced analysis by the greatest living Lermontov specialist; with extensive quotations from secondary literature, plus bibliography.

————, et al., eds. *M. Iu. Lermontov: Seminarii*. Leningrad: Uchpedgiz, 1960. Suggested series of research topics with appropriate bibliography; limited to Russian materials. For use in Soviet colleges and universities.

Mersereau, John, Jr. *Mikhail Lermontov*. Carbondale: Southern Illinois University Press, 1962. A revised doctoral dissertation. Not a "life and works"; ignores the poetry and concentrates on the prose fiction, particularly *A Hero*. Basically sensible, but derivative: relies heavily on Soviet secondary sources and interpretations. Has endnotes but no bibliography.

Mikhailova, E. *Proza Lermontova*. Moscow: Khud. literatura, 1957. Remains the most thorough, detailed, and balanced study of Lermontov's prose fiction.

Turner, C. J. G. *Pechorin*. Birmingham, England: University of Birmingham, 1978. Ponderously written, overly detailed; loses sight of the wood.

Udodov, V. T. *M. Iu. Lermontov*. Voronezh: Voronezh University Press, 1973. Not a "life and works," but a series of chapters devoted to the relationship of Lermontov's personality to his works (the psychology of creativity), to *The Demon* (including an exhaustive discussion of the various texts), to *A Hero*, and to several lyrics. Informative, but much too long and verbose.

2. Collections of Articles

Literaturnoe Nasledstvo, vols. 43–44. M. Iu. Lermontov, Part I. Moscow: Akademiia nauk SSSR, 1941.

Literaturnoe Nasledstvo, vols. 45–46. M. Iu. Lermontov, Part II. Moscow: Akademiia nauk SSSR, 1948.

Tvorchestvo M. Iu. Lermontova. Edited by U. R. Fokht. Moscow: "Nauka," 1964.

M. Iu. Lermontov: Issledovaniia i materialy. Edited by M. P. Alekseev, A. Glasse, and V. E. Vatsuro. Leningrad: "Nauka," 1979. Some important articles and materials, with illustrations. The volume is chiefly notable for the review of the Vereshchagina albums (now located in the library of Columbia University) and other albums belonging to the Baron von Koenig-Warthausen in the Federal Republic of Germany. The American scholar Antonia Glasse provided the necessary assistance and contributes an important article, "Lermontov i E. A. Sushkova," in which she demonstrates that a number of poems, formerly thought to be original, in fact are translations or adaptations from Byron. These discoveries are re-

corded, without acknowledgment, in the four-volume collection
(1979–81).

Lermontovskaia Entsiklopediia. Edited by V. A. Manuilov. Moscow: Sov-
etskaia Entsiklopediia, 1981. Large format, richly illustrated, this
magnificent volume will tell you everything you have ever wanted
to know about the factual background to Lermontov's life and
works.

Index